THE FOUR LAST THINGS

DEATH, JUDGMENT,
HELL AND HEAVEN

REVEREND MARTIN VON COCHEMB O.S.F.C.

AETERNA PRESS

PUBLISHED BY AETERNA PRESS.
COVER DESIGN BY AETERNA PRESS.

FATHER MARTIN VON COCHEM WAS BORN AT COCHEM, ON THE MOSELLE, IN THE YEAR 1625, AND DIED AT WAGHAUSEL IN 1712.

"REMEMBER THY LAST END, AND THOU SHALT NEVER SIN."
HOLY REDEEMER LIBRARY

NIHIL OBSTAT:
THOMAS L KINKEAD,
CENSOR LIBORIUM

IMPRIMATUR:
MICHAEL AUGUSTINE.
ARCHBISHOP OF NEW YORK (NEW YORK OCTOBER 5, 1899)

PRINTED BY BENZIGER BROTHERS, NEW YORK.

ISBN–13: 978–1–78516–340–1

AVAILABLE AS AN E–BOOK:
WWW.AETERNAPRESS.COM

CONTENTS

PART III

PART IV

PART I

ON DEATH

I. On the Terrors of Death

IT appears to me unnecessary to say much about the terrors of death. The subject has been sufficiently enlarged upon by various writers; besides, every one knows and feels for himself that life is sweet and death is bitter. However old a man may be, however broken in health, however miserable his circumstances, the thought of death is an unwelcome one. There are three principal reasons why all sensible people fear death so much:

First, because the love of life, the dread of death is inherent in human nature. Secondly, because every rational being is well aware that death is bitter, and the separation of soul and body cannot take place without inexpressible suffering. Thirdly, because no one knows whither he will go after death, or how he will stand in the Day of Judgment.

It will be well to explain the second and third of these reasons rather more fully, in order on the one hand that those who lead a careless life may perhaps be awakened thereby to a fear of death, and learn to avoid sin, and on the other that each one of us may be warned to prepare for death, lest we be overtaken by it unawares. Every one shrinks instinctively from death, because it is bitter, and painful beyond description to human nature. The soul of man is subject to many anxieties, apprehensions and sorrows, and the body is subject to pain and sickness of all kinds, yet none of these pains can be compared to the agony of death. A man who loses his good name and his property feels acute grief, but he does not die of it. All suffering and sickness, all grief and anguish, however terrible, is less bitter than death. Hence we see death to be a mighty monarch, the most cruel, the most relentless, the most formidable enemy of mankind. Look at a man wrestling with death, and you will see how the tyrant overpowers, disfigures, prostrates his victim. Now why is death so hard, so terrible a thing?

It is because the soul has to separate itself from the body. Body and soul were created for each other, and so intimate is their union that a parting between them seems almost impossible. They would endure almost anything rather than be torn asunder.

The soul is fearful of the future, and of the unknown land to which she is going. The body is conscious that as soon as the soul departs from it, it will become the prey of worms. Consequently the soul cannot bear to leave the body, nor the body to part from the soul. Body and soul desire their union to remain unbroken, and together to enjoy the sweets of life.

In one of his epistles to St. Augustine, St. Cyril, Bishop of Jerusalem, relates what was told him by a man who had been raised from the dead. Amongst other things, he said: "The moment when my soul left my body, was one of such awful pain and distress that no one can imagine the anguish I then endured. If all conceivable suffering and pain were put together they would be as nothing in comparison with the torture I underwent at the separation of soul and body." And to emphasize his words, he added, addressing St. Cyril: "Thou knowest that thou hast a soul, but thou knowest not what it is. Thou knowest that beings exist called Angels, but thou art ignorant of their nature. Thou knowest also that there is a God, but thou canst not comprehend His being. So it is with everything that has not corporeal shape; our understanding cannot grasp these things. In like manner it is impossible for thee to understand how I could suffer such intense agony in one short moment." And if some people apparently pass away most peacefully, this is because nature, exhausted by suffering, has no longer the force to struggle with death.

We know from the testimony of Our Redeemer Himself that no agony is like the agony of death. Although throughout the whole course of His sorrowful Passion, He was tortured in a terrible manner, yet all the martyrdom He endured was not to be compared with what He suffered at the moment of His death. This we gather from the Gospels.

Nowhere do we find that at any period of His life the greatness of the pains He bore extorted from Our Lord a cry of anguish. But when the moment came for Him to expire, and the ruthless hand of death rent His Heart asunder, we read that He cried out with a loud voice, and gave up the ghost. Hence it is evident that at no period of the Passion did Christ suffer so acutely as at the most painful separation of His sacred soul from His blessed body.

In order that mankind might at least in some measure understand how terrible was the death Christ died for us, He ordained that we, at our dissolution, should taste something of the bitterness of His death, and experience the truth of the following words of Pope St. Gregory: "Christ's conflict with death represented our last conflict, teaching us that the agony of death is the keenest agony that man has ever felt or will ever feel. It is the will of God that man should suffer so intensely at the close of his life, in order that we may recognize and appreciate the magnitude of Christ's love for us, the inestimable benefit He has conferred on us by enduring death for our sakes. For it would have been impossible for man fully to know the infinite love of God, unless he too had drunk to some extent of the bitter chalice which Christ drank."

In this passage from the writings of the holy Pope Gregory we are taught that Christ ordained that all men in the hour of their dissolution should suffer the like pains which Christ suffered for us in His last agony, in order that they may gain some knowledge, by their own experience, of the terrible nature of the death He endured for us, and the great price He paid for our ransom. How painful, how terrible, how awful death will be for us, if our death is in any degree to resemble Christ s most agonizing death!

How severe a conflict is before us poor mortals! What torments await us at our last hour! One is almost inclined to think it would have been preferable never to have been born, than to be born to suffer such anguish. But it is thus that Heaven is to be won, and through this narrow gate alone can we enter into Paradise. Wherefore, O Christian, accept your destiny cheerfully, and form a steadfast resolution to bear unmurmuringly the bitterness of death. For it is a great merit to yield up one's life the life every man loves so well and submit with a ready and willing mind to the pangs of death. And for the purpose of encouraging you to gain merit in your last moments, let me counsel you to make the following determination to suffer death bravely.

RESOLUTION

O God of all justice, who hast ordained that since the Fall of our first parents all men should die, and also that it should be the lot of many amongst us to taste in their death something of the pains Thy Son endured at the hour of His death, I submit most willingly to this Thy stern decree. Although life is sweet to me, and death appears most bitter, yet out of obedience to Thee I voluntarily accept death with all its pains, and am ready to yield up my soul whenever, wherever, in what way or mannersoever it may please Thy divine providence to appoint. And since Thou hast made death so bitter to man, in order that we may feel to a certain extent by our own experience how painful a death Thy beloved Son underwent for our sakes, I willingly accept the penalty of death, that I may at least at my latter end know something of the pains my blessed Lord suffered on my account. In honour, therefore, of His bitter Passion and death, I now cheerfully subject myself to whatever sufferings I may be called upon to pass through at the moment of my departure, and declare my determination to bear them with all the constancy of which I am capable. I pray that this resolution on my part may be pleasing in Thy sight, and that Thou wilt give me grace to bear my last agony with patience. Amen.

II. On the Assaults of Satan at the Hour of Death

ALTHOUGH death is in itself most bitter, yet its bitterness is not a little enhanced by the vivid remembrance of the sins of our past life, by the thought of the judgment to come, of the eternity before us, and by the assaults of Satan. These four things fill the soul with such terror, that it would infallibly despair unless strengthened by the help of God.

We will enter into some explanation of each of these four things, and also indicate some means of combating the fears they inspire.

With regard to the assaults of Satan, know that the all–just God permits him to have great power to assail us at the hour of death ; not indeed for our perdition, but for our probation. Before expiring the Christian has yet to prove that nothing can avail to make him forsake his God. For this reason the evil enemy employs all the power he has received, and brings all his forces to bear upon a man when he is dying, in the hope of causing him to sin, and thrusting him down to Hell. During our whole lifetime he attacks us fiercely, and neglects no means whereby he may deceive us. But all these persecutions do not bear comparison with the final onslaught with which he endeavours to overcome us at the last. Then he raves and rages, like a roaring lion, seeking whom he may devour.

This we learn from the following passage in the Apocalypse (xii. 12): "Woe to the earth and to the sea, because the devil is come down unto you, having great wrath, knowing that he hath but a short time." These words bear a special application for the dying, against whom the devil conceives a great wrath, and whom he makes every effort to seduce. For he knows full well that if he does not get them into his power now, he will never again have the chance of doing so. Hear what St. Gregory says on this point:

" Consider well how terrible is the hour of death, and how appalling the remembrance of our evil deeds will be at that time. For the spirits of darkness will recall all the harm they have done us, and remind us of the sins which we have committed at their instigation. They will not go to the death bed of the godless only, but they will be present with the elect, striving to discover something sinful whereof to accuse them. Alas ! how will it fare with us hapless mortals in that hour, and what can we say for ourselves, seeing how innumerable are the sins to be laid to our charge? What can we answer to our adversaries, when they place all our sins before us, with the object of reducing us to despair?"

The evil spirits will tempt their unhappy victim at the moment of death on various points, but especially in regard to the sins into which he has most frequently fallen. If during his lifetime he has cherished hatred towards any one, they will conjure up before his dying eyes the image of that person, rehearsing all he did to injure him, in order to revive the flame of hate towards that enemy, or kindle it anew. Or if any one has transgressed against purity, they will show him the accomplice of his sin, and strive to awaken the guilty passion felt for that individual. If he has been troubled with doubts concerning faith, they recall to his mind the article of belief which he had difficulty in accepting, representing it to him as untrue. If a man has a tendency to pusillanimity, the evil spirits encourage it in him, that they may perchance rob him of his hope of salvation. The man who has sinned through pride, and boasted of his good works, they seek to ensnare by flattery, assuring him that he stands high in the favour of God, and all he has done cannot fail to secure him a place in Heaven. Again, if in his lifetime a man has given way to impatience, allowing himself to be angry and irritated by every trifle, they make his illness appear most irksome to him that he may become impatient, and rebel against God for having sent upon him so painful a malady.

Or if he has been tepid and indevout, without fervour in prayer or assiduity in his religious exercises they try to maintain in his soul this state of apathy, suggesting to him that his physical weakness is too great even to allow him to join in the prayers his friends read to him. Finally, they tempt those who have led a godless life, and repeatedly fallen into mortal sin, to despair, representing their transgressions to be so great as to be past forgiveness. In a word, the spirits of evil assail mortals at the moment of death most fiercely at their most vulnerable point, just as a skillful general will storm a fortress on the side where he perceives the ramparts to be weakest.

But the devils do not always confine themselves to tempting a man in regard to his chief failings and predominant faults; they frequently tempt him to sins of which he has not hitherto been guilty. For these crafty foes spare no pains to deceive the dying, and if they fail in one way, they attempt to succeed in another. These temptations are of no ordinary character. They are sometimes so violent that it is impossible for weak mortals to resist them without supernatural assistance. If it is all that any one in good health can do to withstand the assaults of the devil, and even such a one is often overcome by them, how difficult must it be for one who is enfeebled by sickness to struggle against foes so formidable!

On this point a pious writer says: "Unless the dying man has, previous to his last illness, armed himself against these attacks, and accustomed himself to do battle with his spiritual adversaries, he stands a poor chance of prevailing against them at the moment of death. If he does so, it will be only through the assistance of almighty God, of our blessed Lady, of his guardian Angel, or of one of the Saints. For our merciful God and His Angels and blessed Saints do not abandon the Christian in the hour of his direst need; they hasten to his help, that is, provided he is deserving of their aid." In order to prepare one s self before one s last illness to combat these temptations, it will be advisable to recite with due devotion the following prayer:

O Jesus, compassionate Redeemer of mankind, I recall to mind the threefold temptation Thou didst undergo from the evil enemy, and I pray Thee through the glorious victory Thou didst obtain over him, to stand by me in my last conflict and fortify me against all his temptations. I know that in my own strength I cannot contend against so powerful a foe, and I must assuredly be vanquished unless Thou, or Thy blessed Saints, grant me timely assistance. Therefore I now earnestly implore Thy help and that of Thy Saints, and propose to arm myself to the best of my ability by Thy grace, to meet the temptations that await me. I promise now, before Thee and the holy Angels and blessed Saints, that I will never voluntarily expose myself to any temptation, of whatever nature it may be, but with the help of Thy grace I will combat it vigorously. Amen.

III. On the Apparition of the Spirits of Darkness

BESIDES what has been already mentioned, the terrible appearance of the evil spirits makes death yet more alarming to us. It is the opinion of many of the Fathers, that every one, when expiring, sees the evil enemy, at any rate at the moment of drawing his last breath, if not before. How appalling this sight is, and with what terror it must inspire the dying, exceeds the power of words to declare. It is related of Brother Giles that one day, when he was praying in his cell, the devil appeared to him in so frightful a shape, that the Brother lost the power of speech, and thought his last hour had come. As his lips could not utter a sound, he raised his heart in humble supplication to God, and the apparition vanished. Afterwards, when relating what had befallen him to his brother–monks, he trembled from head to foot as he described the hideous aspect of –the adversary of mankind. Then going to St. Francis, he asked him this question: "Father, have you ever seen anything in this world the sight of which was so horrible that it was enough to kill one to behold it?" And the Saint replied: "I have indeed seen such a thing; it is none other than the devil, whose aspect is so loathsome that no one could gaze upon it even for a short time and live, unless God specially enabled him to do so."

St. Cyril also, writing to St. Augustine, says that one of the three men who were raised from the dead told him: "As the hour of my departure drew nigh, a multitude of devils, countless in number, came and stood about me. Their forms were more horrible than anything imagination can conceive. One would rather be burnt in the fire than be compelled to look upon them. These demons ranged themselves around me, and reproached me with all the misdeeds I had ever done, thinking to drive me to despair. And in fact I should have given way before them, had not God in His mercy come to my succour."

Here we have the testimony of one who actually had learnt by his own experience how frightful the appearance of the evil enemy is, and who declares that nothing can be more horrible than the form the devil assumes.

O my God! how overwhelming the terrors that will take possession of the hapless individual who lies at the point of death when the infernal dragon appears, full of rage, and threatening to swallow him up in his fiery jaws.

In this hour of supreme distress, send my guardian Angel to me, O God, I pray Thee, that he may drive away the evil enemy, otherwise I shall infallibly fall into despair and lose all hope of my salvation.

O most blessed Virgin Mary! who didst crush the head of the serpent, be with me in the hour of my death and do not permit the presence of the cruel adversary to cause my eternal perdition.

IV. On the Fear of Hell

DEATH is rendered yet more bitter to us by the fear of Hell and the clear view of eternity before us. For when we are dangerously ill, and death stares us in the face, the terror which fills us at the prospect of eternity is so overwhelming, that we are filled with fear. For we see plainly that in a few days a few hours perhaps we must enter eternity, and we know not what awaits us there. The dread lest we should be lost everlastingly is so great as to cause us to shudder.

Moreover, the alarm that tortures us is not a little augmented by the remembrance of the sins whereby we have oftentimes deserved Hell; for no man can be certain whether he has done penance aright, and whether he has really obtained pardon. This is explained by a passage from the writings of the aforementioned Pope St. Gregory, who describes this fear in the following words:

"The just man who is truly concerned about his eternal salvation will from time to time think of his future Judge. He will meditate before death overtakes him upon the account he will have to give of his life. If there are no great sins wherewith his conscience reproaches him, he still has cause for alarm on account of the daily sins of which he perhaps takes little heed. For how often do we not sin in thought? It is comparatively easy to avoid evil deeds, but it is a far more difficult matter to keep one s heart free from inordinate thoughts. Yet we read in Holy Scripture: Woe to you that devise that which is unprofitable and work evil in your thoughts (Mich. ii. i). And again: In your heart you work iniquities (Ps. Ivii. 3).

"Hence the just are ever in fear of the awful judgments of God, for they are conscious that all these secret sins will be brought to judgment, as St. Paul says: In that day God shall judge the secrets of men (Rom. ii. 16). And although all his life long a good man will walk in fear of the judgment, yet this fear will notably increase as he draws near to the end of his days. It is said of Our Lord, that when the time of His death approached, He began to be sorrowful and to fear, and being in an agony, He prayed the longer. Was not this intended to teach us how it would be with us in our latter end, and what distress and anguish would overwhelm us?"

Such are the words of Pope St. Gregory, calculated to inspire not only sinners, but also the just with fear, since, as the Saint says, even those who are not conscious of having committed any grievous sins, are yet full of apprehension in regard to the sentence that will be passed on them. If the just are not devoid of alarm, what can we poor sinners do, who know ourselves to be guilty of many and manifold transgressions, and who every day add sin to sin? What will become of us? What can we do? Is there no means we can employ to obtain mercy of God? I know no better counsel than that which Christ Himself gives us in the words: "Watch ye therefore, praying at all times, that you may be accounted worthy to escape all these things that are to come, and to stand before the Son of man" (Luke xxi. 36).

Since Christ points out to us prayer as the best and easiest means, let each one faithfully follow this exhortation and diligently call upon almighty God and His Blessed Mother, and all the Saints, imploring them day by day to protect him, and commending to them his latter end.

V. On the Judgment

ABOVE and beyond all that we have hitherto considered as contributing to make death terrible to us, is the thought that we must stand before the judgment seat of God, and give an account of all we have done and left undone. How awful this judgment is, we learn from these words of St. Paul: "It is a fearful thing to fall into the hands of the living God" (Heb. x. 31). For if it is very alarming even to fall into the hands of an angry man, how much more terrible will it be to fall into the hands of an omnipotent God!

All the Saints trembled in anticipation of the sentence that would be passed on them by God, for they well knew how exceedingly severe His judgments are. The Royal Psalmist says: "Enter not into judgment with Thy servant, O Lord, for in Thy sight no man living shall be justified" (Ps. cxlii. 2).

And holy Job exclaims: "What shall I do if God arise to judge me? What am I that I should answer Him? I cannot answer Him one for a thousand."

Again St. Paul says: "I am not conscious to myself of anything, yet am I not hereby justified; but He that judgeth me is the Lord" (i Cor. iv. 4). We read also in the lives of the Fathers that the holy Abbot Agathon was overwhelmed with fear as his end drew near. His brethren said to him: "Why shouldst thou be afraid, reverend Father, thou hast led so pious a life?" But he answered them: "The judgments of God are very different from the judgments of man." The holy Abbot Elias used likewise to say: "There are three things that I fear. First I dread the moment when my soul has to leave my body; secondly, the moment when I must stand before the tribunal of God; thirdly, the moment when sentence is passed upon me." No one can fail to concur in the saying of this saintly man, for indeed, beside the general judgment, there is nothing so much to be apprehended as these three things. All good and holy men have feared them, all do fear them. Those who do not fear them, prove that they know very little about them, or have meditated scarcely at all upon them. For the benefit of one who may be so unenlightened, I will give a brief instruction on the subject.

Consider, first of all, what a strange new sensation it will be for thy soul, when she finds herself separated from the body, in an unknown world.Hitherto she has known no existence apart from the body; now she is suddenly separated from it.

Hitherto she was in time; now she has passed into eternity.

Now for the first time her eyes are opened, and she sees clearly what eternity is, what sin is, what virtue is, how infinite is the being of the Deity, andhow wondrous is her own nature.

All this will appear so marvellous to her that she will be almost petrified with astonishment. After the first instant of wonder, she will be conducted before the tribunal of God, that she may give an account of all her actions; and the terror that will then seize upon the unhappy soul surpasses our powers of conception.

No wonder the hapless sinner shrinks from appearing before a tribunal where he will be convicted of all his misdeeds and severely punished for them! Would he not rather be thrown into a dark dungeon, and be fed on bread and water, than have to stand before this judgment seat and be put to open shame?

If it is so hateful to a criminal to be brought before an earthly magistrate, well may the poor soul quake with fear when she is introduced into the presence of God, the strict and omniscient Judge, and required to give the most accurate account of all the thoughts, words, deeds and omissions of her past life. Holy Job acknowledges this when he says: "Who will grant me this, that Thou mayst protect me in Hell, and hide me till Thy wrath pass" (Job xiv. 13). Observe that even the patient Job would rather lie in a darksome pit, and be concealed in a gloomy, sombre cave, than appear before the countenance of an angry God.

There are six things which strike terror into the soul, when she is summoned to the particular judgment.

(1) The soul fears because she knows her Judge to be omniscient; that nothing can be concealed from Him, nor can He be in any way deceived.

(2) Because her Judge is omnipotent; nothing can withstand Him, and no one can escape from Him.

(3) Because her Judge is not merely the most just, but the most strict of judges, to whom sin is so hateful that He will not allow the slightest transgression to pass unpunished.

(4) Because the soul knows that God is not her judge alone, but also her accuser; she has provoked Him to anger, she has offended against Him, and He will defend His honour and avenge every insult offered to it.

(5) Because the soul is aware that the sentence once uttered is irrevocable; there is no appeal for her to a higher court, it is useless for her to complain of the sentence. It cannot be reversed, and whether adverse or favourable she must needs accept it.

(6) The most powerful reason of all why the soul fears to appear before the judgment seat is because she knows not what the sentence of the Judge will be. She has far more cause to fear than to hope. And all thought of help is now over. Forever, forever lost; forever, forever damned!

These six points fill the soul with such unspeakable anguish and terror, that were she mortal instead of immortal, she would be willing to die the most cruel and violent death as a means of escape.

Consider, furthermore, in what form thou wilt appear before thy Judge, and how thou wilt be put to confusion on account of thy sins. If a man in punishment of his evil deeds were sentenced to be stripped to the skin in presence of a whole multitude, how greatly ashamed he would feel! But if some loathsome and disgusting sore upon his body were thus disclosed to sight, he would be still more ashamed. Thus will it be with thee, when thou standest before thy Judge in the presence of many hosts of Angels. Not merely will all thy wrong doings, thy thoughts, words and works be revealed, but all thy evil propensities will be made manifest to thee, and thou wilt be put to terrible shame because of them.

Thou canst not deny that these evil proclivities cling to thee, for art thou not given to anger, impatience, revenge, hatred, envy, pride, vanity, sensuality, sloth, greediness, self–love, avarice, worldliness and all malice ? These and other bad tendencies cleave to thy soul, and disfigure it so frightfully, that after death thou wilt be alarmed at the sight of thy own soul, and heartily ashamed of all the stains upon it.

Next consider in what manner thy holy Judge will receive thee, when thou appearest before Him not merely laden with a countless multitude of sins, but in a state of indescribable impurity. Thou wilt stand before Him in the greatest confusion, not knowing which way to look. Beneath thy feet Hell lies; above thee is the angry countenance of thy Judge. Beside thee thou seest the demons who are there to accuse thee. In thy own interior thou beholdest all thy sins and misdeeds. It is impossible to hide thyself; and yet this exposure is intolerable.

This would be a fitting time to expound how the evil enemy will accuse thee, how he will bring all thy sins to light and call down upon them the vengeance of God; and also how the just God will demand the most accurate account of all thy actions.

But this has so often formed the theme of preachers, that, for the sake of brevity, I will not enlarge on this part of my subject, but conclude with the following anecdote.

Two intimate friends agreed together that which ever of the two should die first, should appear to the survivor, provided he was permitted by God to do so. When at length one was removed by death, faithful to his promise he appeared to his friend, but with a sad and woebegone aspect, saying: "No man knows! no man knows! no man knows!"

"What is it that no one knows?" his friend asked.

And the spirit answered: "No one knows how strict are the judgments of God, and how severe His chastisements!"

These things being so, what does it behoove us to do, in order not to fall into the hands of a wrathful Judge? I can give thee no better counsel than this: Repent of thy sins, make a sincere confession, amend thy ways, and begin to think seriously about thy eternal salvation. Whilst thou art still in good health think sometimes of death, and prepare thyself for it. Do not postpone this until old age comes upon thee, or a mortal sickness overtakes thee. There is no greater, no more important art upon earth than the art of dying a good death. Upon this thy whole eternity depends; an eternity of surpassing felicity or of unutterable torment. Only one trial is accorded thee; if thou dost not stand this one trial, all is lost, an eternity of misery is before thee. And if thou hast not learned this all–important art in thy lifetime, when thou art well and strong, how canst thou practise it to thy eternal gain when upon thy death–bed? It will be utterly impossible for thee to do so unless God works a miracle of mercy on thy behalf. Thou canst not reckon upon this; God has not promised it nor hast thou deserved so great a favour, Therefore let me entreat thee to follow my friendly counsel, and prepare thyself frequently for death whilst in full health and strength; for this is the only means whereby thou mayst hope to become proficient in the art of dying well, and pass successfully through the one trial that awaits thee, by which thy eternal destiny will be determined.

PART II

THE LAST JUDGMENT

I. On the Signs that shall Precede the Last Judgment

JESUS CHRIST, the Judge of the living and the dead, who at His first coming appeared upon the earth in all stillness and tranquillity, under a gentle and attractive form, will come again the second time to judgment with great majesty and glory.

In order that His advent may not find us unprepared, He will send beforehand many and terrible signs to warn us to abandon our sinful life. Of these signs He Himself says: "There shall be signs in the sun, and in the moon, and in the stars; and upon the earth distress of nations, men withering away for fear and expectation of what shall come upon the whole world. For there shall be then great tribulation, such as hath not been from the beginning of the world until now, neither shall be. And unless those days had been shortened, no flesh should be saved." What an awful announcement! What a terrible prophecy!

Could there be any more terrible prediction made to us than this which comes from the lips of eternal Truth? When God was about to destroy the city of Jerusalem, He announced its downfall by several signs. A comet, resembling a fiery sword, blazed over the city, and hosts of armed warriors were seen contending in the air. Jerusalem might at the last moment have interpreted aright these signs and done penance unto salvation. But Jerusalem knew not the time of its visitation. If God caused such wondrous signs to appear before the destruction of one single city, will He not announce the approaching end of the world, and the chastisements that are to come upon it, by awful and terrific signs? There is therefore every reason to believe, that a considerable time before the Last Day, fearful signs will appear in all lands in the Heavens. This Christ appears to indicate in the words: "There shall be signs in the sun, and in the moor, and in the stars; men withering away for fear, and expectation of what shall come upon the whole world." These signs will become more numerous day by day, and men will be struck with such terror, that if God did not shorten those days, even the very elect would begin to despair. Then, as St. Jerome says, the Heavens will be overcast with heavy clouds, and a dreadful tempest will arise.

The force of the wind will carry the inhabitants of the earth off their feet, and whirl them aloft in the air; trees will be uprooted, houses unroofed. Long peals of thunder will resound in the Heavens, the flashes of lightning, like serpents of fire, will light up the sky, and with their forked tongues, playing about the dwellings of mankind, will kindle a general conflagration, amid the crash of thunder. The waters of the ocean will be so agitated that their waves will rise mountain–high, towering almost to the clouds. The roaring and raging of the storm–swept billows will last for some time. All the beasts of the earth will lift up their voice, and their dismal howls will fill the air, so that the hearts of men will stand still for terror.

Yet this is but the beginning of sorrow, Our Lord tells us. What will next occur He describes in these words: "Immediately after the tribulation of those days, the sun shall be darkened, and the moon shall not give her light, and the stars shall fall from Heaven, and the powers of Heaven shall be moved."

This darkening of the sun will take place in the full light of midday. And as its golden rays enlightening the face of nature rejoice both man and beast, so the sudden withdrawal of its light will cause sorrow and distress to the whole of creation And this all the more, because the moon will cease to shine, and her gentle, peaceful light will no longer illuminate the shades of night. All the stars also which bespangle the firmament and cast a glimmering to earth, will disappear from their accustomed place. This awful darkness will strike such alarm and anguish to the heart of all living creatures, both men and brutes, that the mourning and lamentation will be universal.

With the wail of distress ascending from the dwellers upon earth, the howls of the evil spirits in the air will mingle in hideous concert, for they will perceive from these signs that the Day of Judgment is at hand; they know that they will soon have to appear before the rigorous tribunal of God; they know they will be cast down to Hell for all eternity. Hence their fury, their rage, and frantic raving.

Here we may repeat the words spoken by Christ: "This is but the beginning of sorrow," and we may add, there will be no end to it. For after the terrific darkness all will be upset and in disorder, and the elements will be let loose, so that men will fear lest the Heavens should fall and the earth sink from beneath their feet. This is what Christ means when He says: "The powers of Heaven shall be moved and the stars shall fall from Heaven." For in accordance with the Divine will, the firmament with all its stars, the sun with its attendant planets, the atmosphere with its veil of clouds, will be so mightily shaken and made to tremble, that appalling sounds of crashing, breaking, fearful explosions, will everywhere be heard. The stars will be driven from their orbits, and thus the great powers of Heaven will conflict with one another.

What will the feelings be of the man who lives through events such as these? How all mankind, all created beings, will mourn! Christ Himself tells us this will be so: "Upon earth will be distress of nations by reason of the confusion of the roaring of the sea and of the waves; men withering away for fear, and expectation of what shall come upon the whole world" (Luke xxi. 25, 26). And in another place He says: "There shall be then great tribulation, such as hath not been from the beginning of the world until now, neither shall be. And unless those days had been shortened, no flesh should be saved" (Matt. xxiv. 21, 22). Our Lord could have used no stronger expression to describe the utter misery of unhappy mortals, than by saying, they shall wither away for fear, and apprehension of the things that are yet to come upon the world. How is it possible for the men who shall be alive at that time not to despond, not to despair, in presence of such fathomless misery? Even the faith and courage of an apostle would be sorely tried to bear up against such unspeakable wretchedness. All men will have the appearance of one who has seen a ghost. Their hair will stand on end, their knees will strike together, they will quake with fear, their terror will deprive them of the power of speech, their hearts will die within them for tribulation, they will lose reason and consciousness, no one will help his neighbour, no one will comfort his neighbour, no one will so much as exchange a word with his neighbour; only they will all unite in weeping and wailing, and fly to hide themselves in the caves of the earth.

When this lamentation has lasted for a time, the God of justice will put an end to their misery, and all that is beneath the firmament of Heaven shall be destroyed by fire. For fire will fall down from Heaven, and ignite everything with which it comes in contact. In many places also flames will spring up out of the ground, and terrify unhappy mortals to such an extent that they will not know how to escape from them. Some will seek shelter in cellars and caverns, others will immerse themselves in rivers and lakes. The devouring flames will spread so fast that the forests will be set on fire, and the towns and villages will be included in the destruction. At length the whole earth will be on fire and a general conflagration will ensue, such as never has been seen or heard of. The heat of the raging flames will be so intense that the stones and rocks will melt, and the sea and all waters upon the earth will boil and hiss.

All men then living, every beast upon the land and every fish in the sea will be destroyed in this universal conflagration. Thus the whole world will be brought to a terrible end, and everything on this earth will be either consumed or purified by the fire. After this has happened, the appearance of the earth will be completely changed.

II. On the Resurrection of the Dead

THE reader will perhaps not take what has been said in the preceding chapter much to heart, because he cherishes the hope that he will not be alive during that awful period. But what we are now about to speak of concerns every one, whoever he may be. Wherefore let him read it attentively and ponder it seriously.

The first event that will follow upon the end of the world is the general resurrection of the dead. All men, whoever they may be, and whenever and wherever they have lived, not excepting infants whose existence has been but one brief moment, will rise again. With the solemn blast of a trumpet God will cause all men to be summoned to the Last Judgment. Concerning this Christ says: "He shall send His Angels with a trumpet and a great voice; and they shall gather together His elect from the four winds, from the farthest parts of the Heavens to the utmost bounds of them" (Matt. xxiv. 31). And St. Paul says: "We shall indeed all rise again, but we shall not all be changed. In a moment, in the twinkling of an eye, at the last trumpet; for the trumpet shall sound, and the dead shall rise again incorruptible: and we shall be changed" (i Cor. xv. 51, 52).

After the vast conflagration God will send out His Angels, who will blow so mighty a blast upon their trumpet, that it will re–echo throughout the whole world. The sound of this trumpet will be so solemn that it will cause the earth to tremble. Its powerful voice will awaken the dead, calling on them: "Arise, ye dead, and come to judgment! Arise ye dead, and come to judgment! Arise, ye dead, and come to judgment!" Loud, continuous, and most solemn will be the blast of that trumpet.

How terrified all the evil spirits and the souls of the lost will be when they hear this call! They will howl and mourn, for the fatal hour has come at last, the hour they have looked forward to so long, and with such unutterable dread. There will be such a commotion in Hell, such raving and raging and fury, that one might imagine the devils were all tearing one another to pieces. "Alas, alas!" they will shriek in their despair. "How can we possibly stand before the countenance of our angry Judge! How can we possibly endure the shame, the agony that will be our portion! Could we only remain here, how gladly would we do so, great as are the torments we have now to endure!" But vain are all their wishes, futile are all their struggles.

They cannot choose, but must obey the voice of the trumpet. The general resurrection begins while its sound still re–echoes over the whole globe. Do not pause to ask how this can be, for we know that it will be so, on the irrefragable authority of God's omnipotence and His word which cannot deceive.

However long ago the body of a man may have crumbled into dust, whatever changes it may have passed through, every portion and every particle will unite to form again the same body which was his during his lifetime. "And the sea gave up the dead that were in it, and death and Hell gave up their dead that were in them" (Apoc. xx. 13).

Consider this solemn truth, O Christian, for it concerns thee closely. As certainly as thou now livest, so certainly wilt thou one day rise again from the grave. Place this awful moment vividly before thee. Even if thou wert pious, and shouldst end thy days in the grace of God, yet, according to the testimony of Holy Scripture and of the Catholic Church, fear and trembling will lay hold upon thee. Considering how inconceivably rigorous God will be in His judgment of men, even the just will have cause to fear in appearing before His tribunal, as we shall presently show. And if good and just men are afraid, what will be the fear that thou, poor sinner, wilt feel, when the trumpet calls thee to judgment! Wherefore amend thy ways, and make thy peace now with thy strict Judge, by works of penance, while there Is yet time. Now in order that thou mayst prepare thyself for that terrible hour of resurrection, we will describe first the resurrection of the good, and then that of the reprobate.

Awakened by the solemn sound of the trumpet all the souls of the just will come down from Heaven, and, accompanied by their guardian Angels, betake themselves to the spot where their remains were interred. The graves will be open, and in them the bodies will be seen lying, incorrupt but yet lifeless. The body of every good man will rest in the grave as if he were asleep; it will be blooming as a rose, fragrant as a lily, shining as a star, fair as an Angel and perfect in every member. What will the soul say when she beholds the body appertaining to her lying before her in such beauty? She will say: "Hail, blessed and beloved body, how I rejoice once more to rejoin thee ! How lovely thou art, how glorious, how pleasing, how fragrant ! Come to me, that I may be wedded to thee for all eternity." Then through the power of God the body will be reunited to the soul, and in that same instant return to life.

O my God, what will be the astonishment of the body when it finds itself alive again, and moulded in so beauteous a form! Soul and body will greet each other lovingly and embrace each other affectionately with heartfelt emotion. The soul will speak thus to the body: "How earnestly I have longed for thee, how I have desired to see this day! Now I will conduct thee to the regions of heavenly bliss that we may rejoice together for evermore." And the body will answer: "Welcome, dearest soul; it is indeed a heartfelt joy to me to be with thee again. The greater the pain our past separation caused me, the greater the delight our present reunion affords."

Then the soul will speak again, and say to the body: "Blessed be thou, my chosen companion, who hast been so faithful to me. Blessed be thy senses and all thy members, for they have ever abstained from evil." And the body will reply: "Be thou rather blessed, O dearest soul, for it was by thy instigation I did so, and thou didst incite me to all that was good. It is to thee that I owe my present felicity, therefore I praise and magnify thee, and I will praise and magnify thee to all eternity."Thus body and soul will rejoice together with inexpressible satisfaction.

Then the holy guardian Angels will congratulate these blessed beings and exult with them over their joyous resurrection. In all cemeteries, and places where many persons are buried, the blessed will arise first with resplendent glorified bodies. That they will take the precedence over the others may be gathered from Christ s words, when He says: "Wonder not at this; for the hour cometh, wherein all that are in the graves shall hear the voice of the Son of God. And they that have done good things shall come forth to the resurrection of life; but they that have done evil, unto the resurrection of judgment" (John v. 28, 29).

And as in every graveyard there are many persons to rise again, and amongst these a considerable proportion will be good and just, imagine the pleasure it will be to them to see one another again, arrayed in such shining glorious bodies.

God grant that I be counted amongst the number of these happy individuals ! How heartily will I thank Him if He grant my request!

The resurrection of the wicked will follow immediately upon that of the just; but oh, how different will it be! In every burying–ground all the lost souls will assemble whose bodies have been interred there, and they will be compelled again to assume them and reunite themselves to them. But what will be the reluctance, the disgust wherewith they will do this ! When the soul sees her own body, she will shrink back from it with the utmost repulsion, so hideous will it be, and she will feel that she had rather go straight to Hell than again unite herself to it. For the bodies of the reprobates will resemble devils more than men, so frightful, so loathsome, so offensive will they be. Yet, however the soul resists and opposes the reunion with her body, now so hideous, she must submit to it, for God compels her to it.

Who can depict the despair that takes possession of the body when, reanimated by the return of the soul, it awakens to a consciousness that it is lost forever. With a shriek of rage it will exclaim: "Woe is me, woe is me to all eternity! Better were it for me a thousand times never to have been born, than to have come to this resurrection of misery!" Then the soul will rejoin: "Thou accursed body, I have already for several hundred years had to endure the torments of Hell, and now I must return with thee to the everlasting burning. Thou art to blame for all this misfortune; I gave thee good counsels, but thou wouldst not follow them. Therefore thou art forever lost. Alas for me, unhappy soul that I am! Alas for me, now and for ever more! Thou hast been the means of bringing me to this endless misery. Therefore I execrate the hour in which I first came to dwell with thee." And then the body will answer the soul after this manner: "O accursed soul, what right hast thou to anathematize me, when thou art thyself the cause of all this wretchedness? Thou shouldst have ruled me more firmly and held me back from evil, for it was with this object that God united thee to me. Instead of associating thyself with me in works of penance, thou didst revel with me in sinful pleasures. It is for me, therefore, to curse thee to all eternity, because thou art the one who hast brought us both to everlasting perdition." Thus soul and body will mutually anathematize each other.

Such are the unhappy circumstances that will attend the resurrection of the bodies of the damned in all graveyards and cemeteries when they leave the grave and enter upon a second life.

And now, reader, endeavour to imagine the shame and confusion which will weigh those poor creatures to the ground when first they see each other again. Husband and wife will meet, brothers and sisters, parents and children, friends and acquaintances; those who have lived in the same town or the same village and have known each other from childhood. Their shame will be so overwhelming that they would prefer to endure any physical torture than be exposed to it. And their bodies will be so hideously ugly, so disgusting in appearance, that they will shudder at the sight of one another. Who can describe the mourning and lamentation that will prevail amongst these hapless creatures! Their misery is indeed unutterable.

Bethink thyself, whoever thou art who readest or hearest this, what awful despair would seize upon thee if thou wert amongst the number of these lost souls. In what piteous tones thou wouldst bewail with them thy hapless fate. "Alas! what have we done? Woe to us most miserable ones; would that we had never been born! Cursed be thou, my wife, who didst provoke me to sin! Cursed be you, my children, who are the cause of my damnation! Cursed be you, my friends and acquaintances, for you were the occasion of this calamity that has come upon me! Cursed forever be all those who have been partners of my life and partners of my sin!"

Think over this, O sinner, and let your hard heart be softened.

Whenever you pass by the cemetery of the place in which you live, remember that perchance thou mayst ere long be laid there to rest in the grave until the general resurrection.

Wherefore make such good use of the brief period of life, that thou mayst be numbered among the just, and arise with them to everlasting felicity, and not with the reprobate to everlasting torments. Pray often thus in thy heart: "O most compassionate Lord Jesus, I implore Thee for the sake of Thy bitter Passion and death, and through the Last Judgment at which Thou wilt be the Judge of the whole world, grant me grace to live in such a manner that at the resurrection I may arise with joy and not with shame." Amen.

III. On the Manner in which the Good and the Wicked will be Conducted to the Place of Judgment

ACCORDING to the generally–received opinion the final judgment will be held in the valley of Josaphat, at no great distance from Jerusalem. This opinion rests upon the words of the prophet Joel: "I will gather together all nations, and bring them down into the valley of Josaphat, and I will plead with them there." And again: "Let the nations come up into the valley of Josaphat, for there will I sit to judge all nations round about" (Joel iii. 2, 12).

It is not difficult to allege a reason why Christ should hold the final judgment there, for it is in the neighbourhood of the spot where He suffered, and is it not just that in the same place He should appear as our Judge? Mount Olivet, the scene of His agony, was also that of His glorious Ascension.

It may, however, be objected, that the valley of Josaphat could not contain the millions and millions of human beings who will be gathered together for judgment. But when a spot is indicated as the probable theatre of the Last Judgment, it does not necessarily follow that all mankind will be crowded into that narrow space.

We will now consider in what manner we shall be assembled for the final judgment. If the good and the evil are found together in the graveyards and elsewhere, that will come to pass which Our Lord predicted: "So shall it be at the end of the world: the Angels shall go out, and shall separate the wicked from among the just" (Matt. xiii. 49). For since the good are laid to rest amongst the wicked, it follows that at the resurrection they will be found amongst the wicked. Accordingly, after the General Resurrection the holy Angels will come and separate the elect from the reprobate. St. Paul, speaking of this, says: "For the Lord Himself shall come down from Heaven with commandment, and with the voice of an archAngel and with the trumpet of God; and the dead who are in Christ shall rise first. Then we who are alive who are left, shall be taken up together with them in the clouds to meet Christ into the air" (i Thess. iv. 15, 16). All the good, that is to say, will be carried on the clouds with splendour and great glory by the Angels to the place of judgment.

Now imagine to thyself what a beautiful sight it will be, when the Saints with their glorified bodies, shining like burnished gold in the sunlight, will be transported through the air, escorted by their guardian Angels! With what exultation and rejoicing will they pass on their triumphal way!

And when they all come together in the valley of Josaphat, they will greet one another lovingly, and embrace one another with mutual joy. Think for a moment, O Christian, how thou wouldst rejoice if thou wert so fortunate as to find thyself amongst the number of the blessed. This happiness is yet within thy reach; if thou dost really desire it with all the strength of thy will, thou wilt be counted in this happy company. Bestir thyself to fulfill all thy duties well and faithfully, and thou too shalt one day join in that glorious and triumphant procession.

We will now consider how the wicked shall be transported to the valley of Josaphat, and what will await them there. Alas! their doom is so sorrowful, that I can scarcely venture to describe it in detail. What will these unhappy sinners think, what will they say, when they see the holy Angels taking the elect from their midst and carrying them with glory and splendour through the air? The Wise Man gives us an insight into their thoughts when he tells us: "These, seeing it, shall be troubled with terrible fear and shall be amazed at the suddenness of the unexpected salvation of the just; saying within themselves, repenting and groaning for anguish of spirit: These are they whom we had sometime in derision, and for a parable of reproach. We fools esteemed their life madness and their end without honour. Behold how they are numbered among the children of God, and their lot is among the Saints" (Wisd. v. 2–5). How it will grieve them to behold those whom they formerly despised so utterly now honoured and beloved by the Angels of God, and conducted by them in glory and triumph to meet Christ. And they who once made such a display of their riches, who despised all their fellow creatures in their arrogant pride, now stand amongst the fallen Angels, poor, miserable, contemned.

When the Angels have escorted all the elect to the valley of Josaphat, they will proceed to drive all the reprobate thither, with the evil spirits that are mingled with them. They will cry with a loud voice: "Away with you, away to judgment! The Judge of the living and the dead commands you to appear before Him."

What a piercing cry of anguish these unhappy creatures will utter ! They will do their utmost to resist the behest of the Angels, but they will struggle in vain; they must obey the command of God s messengers. Together with the evil spirits the damned will be forcibly driven to the place of judgment. What an awful journey! The air is rent with cries of rage. The spirits of darkness, with diabolical malice and cruelty, already vent their spite in tormenting the hapless creatures whom sin has made their victims. Hear the shriek of despair wrung from the wretched beings: "Fools that we were! thoughtless fools! Whither has the path of transgression led us? Alas! it has brought us to the severe, the terribly severe tribunal of God!"

Listen, O sinner, to the sorrowful lamentations and self–accusations of these poor creatures. Beware lest thou too shouldst be of their number. Pray God to preserve you from so shocking a doom, and say: "Most merciful God, remember at how great a price Thou didst purchase me, and how much Thou didst suffer for me. For the sake of that inestimable price do not permit me to be lost, rescue me, number me amongst the sheep of Thy fold. With them I will then praise and magnify Thy loving kindness to all eternity."

IV. How all Men will Await Christ's Coming in the Vale of Josaphat

LET us now contemplate the multitudes gathered together in the place of judgment. All mankind, every human being who has ever lived upon earth, as well as all the rebellious spirits who were cast out of Heaven, will be compelled to appear here before the judgment seat of Christ.

Who can attempt to enumerate these countless multitudes? The number of the earth's inhabitants living at this present moment amounts to about 1,400,000,000. This vast multitude will have disappeared in less than half a century, and another generation, no less numerous, will have taken their place and filled the earth anew. So it will go on and on until the Last Day. What countless hosts there will be arraigned before the judgment seat of Christ!

The good will be all together, rejoicing in the certainty of their eternal salvation. They are adorned with glorious apparel, and shine like the stars of Heaven. They know one another, they greet one another, and exchange mutual congratulations respecting their happy lot.

Not so the wicked. The good stand on the right hand, and they upon the left. Unfortunately the number of the wicked is far, far larger than that of the good. Both before and after the coming of Christ the prince of darkness held sway over a much greater number of subjects than Christ Himself.Alas ! my God, what an immense multitude there will be on the left hand! The mourning and misery amongst them will be so unparalleled that the good who are on the right hand would, were it possible, be deeply touched with compassion.

For all these countless millions of human beings will pour out their excessive sorrow and anguish in piteous lamentations. Awaiting the coming of the supreme Judge, they stand together, apart from the just, full of confusion at their own hideousness, and especially at their sinfulness, now evident to all.

Yet above and beyond all this misery is the consternation that prevails on account of the coming of the Judge; it is beyond the power of words to express. For now these unhappy creatures first become fully aware how terrible are the judgments of God, which they during their lifetime heeded so little. Now for the first time they recognize what a fearful disgrace it is for them to have their sins made manifest in the presence of all the Angels and Saints, in the presence likewise of the devils and of the lost. Now for the first time they are conscious of the awful nature of the sentence that will be passed on them by the Judge whom they have often insolently set at naught. These and many other things contribute to imbue them with such an unutterable dread of the coming of their Judge, that they quake in every limb with terror, and almost swoon away with apprehension and alarm. They will say to one another in plaintive tones: "Alas, what have we done! How terribly we have deceived ourselves ! For the sake of the few and transitory joys of earth, we must undergo an eternity of anguish. What good are all the riches, the voluptuous pleasures, the pride, the honours of the world to us now? We fools have trifled away celestial and eternal goods for the poor and paltry things of earth. Alas, what will become of us when our Judge appears! Ye mountains, fall on us, and ye hills, cover us, for truly it would be less intolerable for us to be crushed under your weight, than to stand before the whole world covered with shame and confusion, and behold the wrathful countenance of the just Judge!"

Unhappy sinner, whoever thou art who readest this book, do not flatter thyself with the vain hope that this description of the misery of the lost is exaggerated. They will complain a thousand times more loudly, and their pain and misery will be unutterable. Avail thyself of the short and precious season of thy earthly existence, do penance, do now all that thou wouldst desire to have done at the Day of Judgment. Ask of God grace to amend thy sinful life, in order that the day of Christ s coming may not be a day of unspeakable terror to thee.

My God, I acknowledge that by my sinful life I have deserved to be banished from Thy presence forever. Yet I sincerely repent of my sins and pray Thee for the grace of a true conversion, so that I may not await Thy coming among the number of the lost. Amen.

V. On the Appearance of Christ's Cross in the Heavens

WHEN all mankind are assembled in the valley of Josaphat, the prediction of Our Lord will be fulfilled: Men withering away for fear, and expectation of what shall come upon the whole earth." For they will be in such anxiety and terror in anticipation of the approaching judgment that, if such a thing were possible, they would faint away. They will look up to the Heavens continually with fear and trembling, and every moment that the coming of the dreaded Judge is delayed will serve to increase their apprehension of this advent. At length the Heavens will be opened, and the sign of Christ s triumphant victory, the sign of the holy Cross, will be carried down by a host of Angels and exhibited to the whole world.

These are Our Lord s words in regard to this mystery: "The powers of Heaven shall be moved, and then shall appear the sign of the Son of man in Heaven, and then shall all tribes of the earth mourn" (Matt. xxiv. 29, 30). The Catholic Church teaches us what this sign will be, which is to appear in Heaven: The sign of the Cross will appear in Heaven, when the Lord shall come to judgment. All the Fathers concur in interpreting this sign which will be displayed in the Heavens as the Cross of Christ. Although the cross whereon Our Lord suffered is now divided into innumerable little pieces, into particles even, yet by Divine power it will once more form a complete whole. It will be carried down from Heaven by the Angels with solemn pomp; and the Angels who bear it will be followed by others, who, as the Angelic Doctor, St. Thomas Aquinas, maintains, will carry all the other instruments of the Passion; that is to say, the pillar, the lance, the scourges, the hammer, the iron glove, the dice, the scarlet robe, the white robe, the seamless tunic, the holy winding–sheet, the vessel containing myrrh and all the other instruments that were employed during the Passion, and the object of this will be to make manifest to the whole world how many and manifold were the pains Christ suffered for our sakes.

Now when all mankind behold the holy cross and all the other sacred instruments of the Passion shining like the sun at midday, for the cross of Christ will gleam with a light of unexampled brilliance, those who are waiting below will stand in trembling fear and woeful lamentation. For the sight of the holy cross and the other instruments of torture will recall to their mind all the grievous pains that Our Lord endured, and indeed in so forcible and vivid a manner, that His whole Passion will seem to be re–enacted before them. Then the bitterest remorse will fill the heart of the wicked. But this remorse, how great and how deep soever it may be, will be futile. It comes too late. This remorse is the companion of despair. In their anguish of soul and their despair they will exclaim with Cain, the fratricide:

"My iniquity is greater than that I may deserve pardon; "or with Judas, who betrayed his Lord and Master: "I have sinned, in betraying innocent blood." Yes, all the lost will concur in exclaiming, "Alas! we have sinned in betraying innocent blood. We have tortured, we have crucified, we have put the Son of God to death by our sins." Then all the tribes of the earth will mourn, for they will perceive how grievously they have offended against God, but the cries of mourning and despair prevailing everywhere will be in vain.

What will the unfortunate heathen say, who have never heard, never known anything about Christ's Passion? They will bitterly bewail and lament their ignorance, saying: "Alas! we unhappy ones, had we but known this, we should never have come to this misery. Had we but known that the great and infinite God did and suffered so much for us, how grateful we should have been to Him, how willingly we would have served Him! We were deluded by our false gods. We saw in them no virtues, only vile and vicious deeds. Against the promptings of conscience we imitated their vices, and hence we are damned. We cannot complain, or think ourselves wronged by the holy and just God, because we are amongst the reprobate. If only we had hearkened to the voice of our conscience, this would not have been our fate."

But what will those say who put Christ to death? Pilate, Caiphas, Annas, the high priest, as well as the Jews who cried: "Crucify Him! " and "His blood be upon us and upon our children," all who took part in the cruel, atrocious crime of crucifying their God, will at the sight of the sacred instruments of the Passion shriek aloud in despair and desire to be annihilated. Execrated and cursed even by the damned, they will stand there, branded as deicides, objects of abhorrence to the whole world.

It is not my intention to discuss what bad Christians, who have blasphemed the Son of God by word or deed, will feel at that time; for brevity's sake I leave thee, reader, to meditate upon it for thyself. Only one thing I would ask of thee; reflect upon this, what thou wouldst say, what thou wouldst most deeply regret, if thou wert amongst the number of the damned, and didst then perceive that thou hadst been the cause of Christ s sufferings and hadst crucified

Him by thy sins. Couldst thou now feel in thy heart something of the contrition which would then pierce thy soul, assuredly thou wouldst never again for the remainder of thy life commit any heinous sin. Couldst thou now mourn over the sufferings of Christ with expressions of such poignant sorrow as would then rise to thy lips, thou wouldst infallibly obtain the remission of thy sins. Wherefore, frequently adore thy crucified Saviour, call to mind His sufferings for thy sake, and recite the following prayer:

O faithful Redeemer of the world, who didst endure such unspeakable sufferings for me, a miserable sinner, I pray Thee let not Thy bitter Passion and Thy death upon the cross be unavailing for me. Impress the remembrance of them deeply upon my heart, that I may have them ever before my mind, and may avoid sin which was the cause of Thy suffering. Thus when Thy cross shall appear bright and shining in the Heavens on the Day of Judgment, may it not be to me a sign of damnation, but of salvation, a sign of Thy mercy and of Thy love. Amen.

VI. On the Advent of the Judge

WHAT we have hitherto heard, O Christian reader, is indeed most fearful and terrible, but it is nothing in comparison with what we are now about to consider. For the coming of the Judge will be so awful, so dreadful, that all that is in Heaven or upon earth will tremble and quake. The power and majesty wherewith He will come is beyond the power of words to describe. In order that we may know something concerning it, and be able to form some conception of it, Christ has Himself foretold His coming in these words: "When the Son of man shall come in His majesty, and all the Angels with Him, then shall He sit upon the throne of His majesty, and all nations shall be gathered together before Him" (Matt. xxv. 31,32). And again: They shall see the Son of man coming in the clouds of Heaven with much power and majesty" (xxiv. 30). Thus we see Our Lord twice asserts that He will come in the clouds of Heaven, attended by all His Angels, in great might and majesty.

Who can depict the greatness of that power, the splendour of that majesty, the countless number of those Angelic hosts! Listen to what the Psalmist says on the subject: "A fire shall go before Him and shall burn His enemies round about. His lightnings have shone forth to the world, the earth saw and trembled. The mountains melted like wax at the presence of the Lord, at the presence of the Lord of the whole earth. The Heavens declared His justice and all people saw His glory" (Ps. xcvi. 3–6). And in another psalm we read: "Out of

Sion the loveliness of His beauty shall shine forth.. . . A fire shall burn before Him, and a mighty tempest shall be round about Him" (xlix. 2). The prophet Isaias also predicts the advent of the Judge in the following terms: "Behold, the Lord will come with fire, and His chariots are like a whirlwind, to render His wrath in indignation and His rebuke with flames of fire" (Is. Ixvi. 15). Moreover, Christ Himself declares: "As lightning cometh out of the east, and appeareth even into the west: so shall also the coming of the Son of man be" (Matt. xxiv. 27).

If such be the manner in which the Judge shall come, if flames of fire proceed from His countenance, if He descends from Heaven in a fiery chariot, armed with wrath against sinners, who but must tremble at His coming ! We shall in fact, all falter and be afraid. Besides the terrors of the Judge Himself, the sight of the innumerable company of Angels that will descend with Him, will inspire us with awe and great alarm. For on that day not one Angel will remain in Heaven; they will all be present as witnesses of the judgment.

Now, theologians maintain that in the lowest choir of Angels the number of Angels is ten times greater than that of all the human beings that have ever existed upon earth. In the second choir there are ten times as many as in the first, in the third ten times as many as in the second, and so on, so that the number of these Angelic beings appears endless. All these Angels, who are pure spirits and therefore invisible to bodily sight, will then appear visible, exceedingly bright and glorious, so that the damned also may see the magnificence of Christ s advent.

St. John in his Apocalypse speaks thus of the hosts of Angels that will attend upon the Judge at His coming: "I saw Heaven opened, and behold a white horse; and He that sat upon him was called faithful and true, and with justice doth He judge and fight. And His eyes were as a flame of fire, and on His head were many diadems; . . . and He was clothed with a garment sprinkled with blood, and His name is called: The word of God." And the armies that are in Heaven followed Him on white horses, clothed in fine linen, white and clean. And out of His mouth proceedeth a sharp two–edged sword, that with it He may strike the nations. And He shall rule them with a rod of iron ; and He treadeth the wine–press of the fierceness of the wrath of God the almighty. And He hath on His garment and on His thigh written : King of kings, and Lord of lords" (Apoc. xix. 11–16).

How we all shall tremble, O my God, when we behold these hosts of celestial spirits with their kingly leader! The prophet Daniel once saw an Angel, and he was so terror–struck at his appearance, that he fell to the ground like one dead. If such an effect was produced on him by the sight of a single Angel, whose errand was one of comfort and consolation, what will become of us, when so many hundreds of thousands of heavenly princes draw nigh to us with wrathful countenances? St. Ephrem, speaking of this says: "The Angels will stand there with a menacing mien, their eyes flashing with the sacred fire of just indignation, roused by the iniquities of mankind."

Now if the sight of the Angels alone, who will come to judgment with the Divine Judge, is so terrible, what will be the fear and dread inspired by the Judge Himself, when He comes in all the wrath of offended justice! As in Heaven there is no greater delight than the contemplation of God, so at the Last Judgment there will be no greater pain than to look upon the angry Judge. Before entering upon an explanation of this, let us see with what majesty Christ will come to judgment.

The advent of Christ will be so terrible that neither man nor Angel is capable of describing it aright. For all that is most calculated to appal the sinner will be here seen, and nothing will be wanting that can enhance the majesty of Christ. When a monarch makes his entry into a town, what pomp and splendour is displayed there ! Strains of lively music mingle with the more solemn peal of bells, salutes are fired, the whole population is astir, every one straining his eyes to see the monarch; first come his servants, then his counsellors, then the nobles of the land; lastly he comes himself, surrounded by a vast multitude of people.

Yet what is all this magnificence the world can offer when compared with the majesty which will attend the coming of the King of kings! Compare a poor ragged beggar–boy with a sovereign prince who enters riding in a chariot of gold, and we have a feeble and insufficient image of the difference that exists between the pomp and splendour of this world and the glory wherewith Christ will come to judgment.

Yet His advent will not merely be grand and glorious beyond measure, it will likewise be awful in its nature. If the graves opened at the blast of the Angel's trumpet, and the sound of that trumpet re–echoed throughout the whole world, what a panic of fear will seize upon mankind when the Angels who precede Christ's triumphal call cause the sound of their trumpets to be heard!

" What," asks St. Augustine, "will become of us on that dreadful day, the Day of Judgment, when the Lord shall descend with His Angels with the sound of trumpets, and the whole earth shall tremble with fear?"

When God came down of old upon Mount Sinai, we read in Holy Scripture: "Now the third day was come and the morning appeared; and behold thunders began to be heard, and lightning to flash, and a very thick cloud to cover the mount, and the noise of the trumpet sounded exceeding loud, and the people that was in the camp feared." And when all the people heard the thunder and the sound of the trumpet, and saw the lightning and the smoke arising from out of the mount, they were terrified, and withdrew to a distance, saying to Moses: "Speak thou to us and we will do all things that the Lord hath commanded, but let not the Lord speak to us lest we die" (Exod. xx. 19).

If all this happened when God came down from Heaven to give His law to the Hebrew nation, and adopt them as His children, what, thinkest thou, O Christian, will be the case when He comes to require an account of the manner in which His commandments have been kept? If the children of Israel were so terrified at the giving of the law that they thought they should die of fear, what cause shall not we mortals, we Christians especially, have to tremble, since we have so often wilfully transgressed the commandments of God!

O God, almighty Judge of all men, Thou wilt descend from Heaven at the Last Day with great power and majesty, to act in Thy character of Judge, and the thought of Thy coming causes me to quake with fear. Inspire me now, I beseech Thee, with salutary fear, so that I may avoid sin, and may not merit to be crushed by Thy just anger. Amen.

VII. On the Manner in which Christ will take His Place on the Judgment–seat

PAY heed, O reader, to what is now coming, and do not imagine that it concerns thee not. Thou wilt most assuredly witness it all one day with thy bodily eyes, and all will be a thousand times more terrible than my pen can depict it.

When Christ, in His chariot of fire, has reached Mount Olivet, He will pause in the air, at such a height that He can be clearly seen by all men, until the Angels have prepared the throne of judgment.

The prophet Daniel thus portrays the scene: "I beheld till thrones were placed, and the Ancient of days sat ; His garment was white as snow and the hair of His head like clean wool; His throne like flames of fire, the wheels of it like a burning fire. A swift stream of fire issued forth from before Him; thousands of thousands ministered to Him, and ten times a hundred thousand stood before Him: the judgment sat and the books were opened" (Dan. vii. 9, 10).

But Christ will not sit in judgment alone; the twelve Apostles will be with Him, according to the promise He gave them: "Amen I say to you, that you who have followed Me, in the regeneration, when the Son of man shall sit on the seat of His majesty, you also shall sit on twelve seats judging the twelve tribes of Israel" (Matt. xix. 28).

Who can give any idea of the magnificence of Christ s throne? It beggars all description.

We read that King Solomon caused a wonderfully beautiful throne to be constructed out of ivory, richly adorned with gold and precious stones. This throne was so magnificent that the inspired writer says of it that in no kingdom of the world had any such work been made. If the judgment–seat of King Solomon was composed of such costly material and fashioned so skilfully, what will be the splendour of the judgment–seat of the King of kings, on which He will sit in His majesty to judge the whole world!

Our Lord speaks of this judgment–seat as a throne of great splendour, when He says: "When the Son of man shall come in His majesty, and all the Angels with Him, then shall He sit upon the seat of His majesty" (Matt. xxv. 31).

Some idea of what the appearance of this throne will be may be gathered from the words which have just been quoted from the prophet Daniel, and also this description given by St. John: "There was a rainbow round about the throne, in sight like unto an emerald.. . . And from the throne proceeded lightnings, and voices, and thunders; and there were seven lamps burning before the throne" (Apoc. iv. 3–5).

Such are the images whereby Holy Scripture portrays the judgment–seat of Christ. Who of all mankind can venture to raise his eyes to this fiery throne? Will it not be more dazzlingly bright than the lightnings and fiery flashes of a tempest?

The Divine Judge will seat Himself upon this throne and His grave countenance will be visible to men and Angels. All created beings will tremble with awestruck reverence. St. John declares this in the Apocalypse: "I saw a great white throne, and One sitting upon it, from whose face the earth and Heaven fled away, and there was no place found for them" (Apoc. xx. 11). In these words the prophet of the New Testament appears to indicate that the Heavens and the earth will not be able to bear to meet the eye of their Judge; that all rational beings, both Angels and men, will quake at the sight of His stern countenance.

That the Angels also will fear and tremble, is asserted by St. Augustine, in the following passage from his writings: "When Our Lord says that the powers of Heaven shall be moved, He alludes to the Angels; for so terrible will the judgment be, that the Angels will not be exempt from fear; they too will tremble and be afraid. For just as when a judge sits in judgment his grave countenance not only strikes terror into the culprits before him, but over–awes the officials standing around, so when all mankind are brought to judgment the celestial ministers will share the universal horror and alarm."

St. John Chrysostom corroborates this statement, when he says: "Every one will then be filled with astonishment, with apprehension, with terror, for even the Angels will be sore afraid."

Many other Fathers of the Church and commentators upon Holy Scripture express a similar opinion.

Now if, according to the opinion of learned and holy men even the Angels will not be without fear in the Day of Judgment, how much greater cause will the Saints have to fear, since they must stand before Christ's tribunal, and give a strict account of all their actions. Yes, it is unmistakably evident, from what St. John says in the Apocalypse, that the blessed Saints are struck with awe and trembling. He describes how Christ appeared to him, and the effect it had upon him. " When I had seen Him, I fell at His feet as dead. And He laid His right hand upon me, saying, Fear not. I am the First and the Last." If the beloved Apostle was so awestruck at the sight of his dear Master and Lord, who had come to console and not to judge him, that he fell at His feet as if dead, and could not summon up courage to rise to his feet until Christ spoke to him in the kindest and most comforting manner, can it be supposed that the Saints will not be terrified on the Day of Judgment, when they behold Christ in His awful majesty and are called upon to give to Him an account of their whole life? And, O poor sinner, how will it then fare with thee, and with all the reprobate, if even the Angels and Saints tremble at the coming of the Judge? Words cannot express the terror and dismay of evil spirits and unrepentant sinners, when they shall behold their Divine Judge on the throne of His majesty, and know that He will rigorously judge and condemn them to Hell for all eternity.

In order to give some idea of the terrible dread and alarm of the fallen Angels and of unhappy sinners, let us hear what Holy Scripture says concerning the appalling exterior of the Judge and the greatness of His anger, in the first chapter of the Apocalypse, where St. John tells us: "I saw the Son of man clothed in a garment down to the feet and girt about the breast with a golden girdle. His head and His hairs were white as white wool and as snow, and His eyes were as a flame of fire, and His feet like unto fine brass, as in a burning furnace. And His voice as the sound of many waters. And from His mouth came out a sharp two–edged sword, and His face was as the sun shineth in His power. Upon His head were many diadems, and He was clothed with a garment sprinkled with blood. He treadeth the wine–press of the fierceness of the wrath of God the almighty, and He hath on His garment and His thigh written: King of kings and Lord of lords."

Meditate upon these wondrous words, O Christian, and picture to thyself thy future Judge in vivid colors. How could His majestic appearance be described more forcibly than in the words we have just quoted?

What must be the splendour of that countenance which is said to shine as the sun at its meridian! what must be the brilliance of those eyes which glow with holy fervour like flames of fire! what the force of that voice which has the sound of a volume of waters! what must be the keenness of that tongue which cuts like a two–edged sword! what a glorious head that must be which is adorned with many costly diadems! How terrible that garment must be to look upon which is sprinkled with blood ! And what the dignity of that regal name: The King of kings and Lord of lords! How frightened we all shall be, what fear and woe will overtake us when our Judge looks upon us! And imagine what the feelings of the damned will be, when they behold the Judge of all their wicked deeds; how they will quail and quake beneath His gaze in the hour of His just wrath!

We shall perhaps form a better conception of what the wrath of God is, if we listen to what the prophet Isaias says concerning it: "Behold the name of the Lord cometh from afar, His wrath burneth, and is heavy to bear; His lips are filled with indignation, and His tongue as a devouring fire; His breath as a torrent overflowing even to the midst of the neck, to destroy the nations into nothing" (Is. xxx. 27, 28).

These are of a truth terrible words. Do they not clearly indicate with what great wrath Christ will manifest Himself to the world ? Well may all unhappy sinners be overwhelmed with terror and dismay and anguish; well may they cry to the mountains to fall on them and the hills to cover them.

Now when the Judge is seated upon the throne of His majesty, all who are assembled in the valley of Josaphat, Angels and devils, the redeemed and the lost, will all have to adore Christ, as St. Paul says: "We shall all stand before the judgment–seat of Christ. For it is written: As I live, saith the Lord, every knee shall bow to Me, and every tongue shall confess to God" (Rom. xiv. 10, 11).

How solemn and how sublime a scene will then be enacted, O my God, when all the millions and thousands of millions of Angels, together with the blessed, in visible form will prostrate themselves upon the ground, and the evil spirits with their unhappy victims, and all the damned, will be forced against their will to adore Christ and acknowledge Him as their God and Judge ! These wretched creatures will fall on their knees, and bend their heads down to the earth, not daring to raise their eyes, lest they should encounter the angry glance of their Judge. They will lament and bewail, filled with unutterable consternation and dismay. Gladly would they have the earth open and swallow them up, nay, they would, if it were possible, cast themselves down into a bottomless abyss rather than suffer such humiliation.

Pause and consider, O sinner, what thy feelings would be if thou wert amid the number of these lost souls; thou wouldst be overwhelmed with sorrow and distress.

St. Vincent relates that a young man of dissolute life once dreamed that he was arraigned before the judgment–seat of God, and required to give an account of his ill–spent life. His terror was so great that it turned his hair perfectly white. If the terrors of the Last Judgment experienced only in a dream were sufficient to turn the colour of that young man s hair, what, thinkest thou, will be the effect they will produce on thee and on me, when we are present, not in a dream, but in reality, at the Last Judgment, and with our bodily eyes we behold our Judge in all His holy indignation?

O most just Judge, look down, I beseech Thee, from Thy throne in Heaven upon me, a poor sinner, and for the sake of Thine infinite compassion be merciful to me in the day of final judgment. I know that I shall not be able to stand in that dread day, but by Thy just sentence I shall be condemned to eternal damnation. Yet I know also that if a sinner implores mercy of Thee in the time of grace, it will not be denied him. Therefore I entreat Thee with deep humility and contrition, through Thy bitter Passion, that Thou wouldst pardon my sins and pass a lenient sentence upon me in the Day of Judgment. Amen.

VIII. On the Reason why Christs Appearance on the Day of Final Judgment will be Terrible, and on the Heinousness of Mortal Sin

THE reader may, perchance, be inclined to ask the reason why Christ, the same Christ who lived amongst us on earth in all gentleness and meekness, should wear so terrible an aspect when He comes to be our Judge? There are a great many reasons why Christ in this capacity should judge mankind with such awful severity. The principal one is because He has been most grievously outraged by the sins of men.

Theologians assert that every mortal sin is in itself an infinite evil, and is an infinite affront to the Divine majesty. It is an offence of such magnitude that neither the tongue of Angels nor of men is capable of describing it. It will be understood, therefore, that as in every mortal sin there is malice of so deep a dye, it must deeply wound the Divine Heart of Jesus, and provoke Him to just anger against the individual who has been guilty of that sin. And in order that it may be more apparent how just the ire of God is, when roused by mortal sin, it will be well to explain more clearly how great is the insult offered to God by wilful sin. Imagine the three Divine persons of the Most Holy Trinity to be on one side, with their infinite treasures of grace and glory, and on the other side the spirit of evil with all the punishments and torments of Hell; and a man standing in the midst betwixt the two, debating within himself whether he should show honour to God by doing His will, or whether he should act in violation of His will, and thereby cause the devil to rejoice. If the man commits the sin, he acts towards God, and God regards his action, exactly as if he uttered these blasphemous words, or others of the same nature:

"I do indeed believe, O God, that I was created by Thine almighty power, redeemed by Thy mercy, made a child of predilection by Thy bounty, I know that Thou hast promised me eternal life, all the sweetest bliss of Heaven. I am also well aware that this accursed Satan, Thy great enemy and mine, is prepared to strip me of all that is good, and hurl me down into everlasting perdition. And yet because Satan tempts me now, because he suggests to me a thought of unchastity, a desire for revenge, a movement of envy, I choose rather to yield to this impulse and thereby render myself deserving of everlasting punishment, than resist and repel the evil suggestion and thus merit Heaven hereafter and spiritual graces now. Therefore, I deliberately and of my own free will, turn from Thee, O God; I follow by choice this hateful demon, whom I obey in preference to Thee. Although Thou art my God and my Lord, although Thou hast forbidden us to transgress Thy law, although sin is an infinite offence against Thee, yet I do not care, I will commit sin all the same, I will not desist because it is an outrage to Thee.

Nay, more, if I could do all that in the malice of my heart I would do, I should rob Thee of Thy God head, I should cast Thee down from Thy throne, and in Thy place I should set up sin, and worship that as my god. I love sin, I desire to revel in it, and find in it my sole happiness."

Such blasphemies as these words express are terrible, and cannot be read without a shudder. Yet every man who wilfully and in defiance of God's law commits a mortal sin is guilty of blaspheming God in the like manner. What wonder, then, that God is so deeply offended by mortal sin. But we have not yet shown the full extent of the malice of sin it goes still farther ; it is doubly offensive to God because the sinner not only manifests contempt for God the Father, he also sets at naught His beloved Son, the Second Person of the Divine Trinity. By every wilful sin he seems to say: "It is true Thou didst become man for me, Thou didst seek for me for three and thirty years, as a sheep that was lost; Thou didst endure hunger and thirst, heat and cold, and all manner of hardships for my sake, whilst Satan has done nothing of the sort for me; on the contrary, he pursues me day and night and strives to ensnare me. In spite of this I prefer to belong to him rather than to Thee. I prefer to please him, and grieve Thee.

"Is it true, O my Redeemer, that for my sake Thou wast torn with scourges, crowned with thorns, fastened with nails to the Cross and put to death amid bitter tortures; yet for all this I offer Thee no thanks. Nay more, although I know that by my sins I scourge Thee, I crucify Thee, I put Thee to death anew, yet I will not forsake my sins; I will trample upon Thy precious blood, I will adore Satan instead of Thee; I will make him my dearest friend and do my utmost to give him pleasure."

Again I ask, are not these utterances blasphemous in the extreme? Do they not show the blackest ingratitude on the part of the sinner towards his Saviour? One can scarcely imagine that a Christian would grieve his Redeemer in so shameful a manner. And yet there are many thousands who, if not in words, yet in deeds, address such language to their Saviour.

In the third place, the audacious sinner outrages and defies the Holy Spirit of God, for his actions are equivalent to expressions such as these: "Thou, O Holy Ghost, hast certainly sanctified my soul, cleansed it in the blood of Christ and beautified it by Thy grace. I know that Thy sanctifying grace is so precious that every soul which is adorned by it thereby becomes a daughter of the heavenly Father, a sister of the Divine Son, a spouse of the Holy Ghost, the dwelling–place of the Most Holy Trinity, a temple of the sovereign Godhead, an heir of eternal felicity, a friend of Angels and Saints, yet what do I trouble myself about these exalted prerogatives, what do I care for this priceless pearl, this costly jewel? Away with them; I will cast this pearl, this jewel to the dogs and swine, to wit, my evil passions. I will sacrifice all to them, I will serve sin and live in sin."

Seest thou not now, O reader, how hateful sin is, how shocking the nature of the sinner, how infinite the offence against God, the contempt of God which is inseparable from sin? Art thou not convinced that God has just cause to feel holy indignation against sin and the slaves of sin, and to condemn the sinner to everlasting damnation?

And if the wrath of God, who is infinite in sanctity and justice, is aroused to such an extent by one single mortal sin, how greatly must He, the just and holy One, be angered and offended by the millions upon millions of shameless and shameful sins daily committed not only by Jews and heathens, but also by

Christians! All this anger, all this sense of outraged dignity at insult offered, which the sinner arouses within the Heart of God, is treasured up until the Day of Judgment. The holy sacrifice of the Mass and the powerful intercession of the Saints as yet restrains the Divine arm from executing vengeance.

But when mankind have filled up the measure of their iniquities, the day of wrath shall come. No one can form a conception of how awful the outpouring of the wrath of God upon sinners will be. In the Psalms we read: "Who knoweth the power of Thy anger, and for Thy fear can number Thy wrath?" (Ps. Ixxxix. ii.)

Woe, then, to us poor sinners ! Then for the first time we shall appreciate aright what we have done and how deeply we have offended God by our grievous sins. The wrath of God is so boundless that neither the Mother of God, nor all the Angels and Saints have any power to diminish or restrain it; it will turn with holy zeal and mete out to every man his deserts with rigorous justice. Hear what the Judge Himself says of this, His wrath, by the mouth of the prophet Ezechiel: "Now, thou son of man, is an end come upon thee, and I will send My wrath upon thee, and I will judge thee according to thy ways, and I will set all thy abominations against thee, and My eye shall not spare thee, and I will show thee no pity" (Ezech. vii. 3, 4).

These are truly terrible words, and the threat they contain is most appalling. Oh, how unsparing will be the judgment to which God, who has been offended by transgressions so innumerable, will summon all mankind.

Alas for me and for thee, if we find ourselves amid the countless multitude of sinners, and God cannot in justice spare us ! What shall we do, that we may not fall into the hands of the angry Judge?

We must abandon the way of iniquity, and now, while there is yet time, make our peace with the Judge whom we have offended. Let us awaken from time to time sincere contrition for our sins, employing these or similar expressions of sorrow:

Most just Judge of the living and the dead, I acknowledge before Thee that I have sinned often and grievously. I have forsaken my Father in Heaven; I have crucified Thee, my Redeemer; I have grieved the Holy Spirit and trifled away His grace. I have done this by the countless sins I have committed in thought, word and deed. Through my transgressions I have incurred the penalty of everlasting death. But since Thou willest not the death of the sinner, but rather that he should do penance and live, let me experience here the effect of Thy justice, which is ever wedded to mercy. All the trials that Thou sendest me in this life I will thankfully receive from Thy hand, and kiss the rod whereby Thou dost chastise me with paternal 1 severity in order that at the Day of

Judgment I may find mercy, and Thou mayst grant me a place in the ranks of Thine elect. Amen.

IX. On the Manner in which the Final Judgment will be Commenced

WHILST the Angels and Saints, besides all the company of the devils and the damned, are prostrate before their Judge in lowly adoration, He will open His lips, and with a loud voice utter these or similar words: "Listen, ye Heavens, to My voice; listen, O earth, to the words that I shall speak; listen, ye Angels, listen, ye demons, listen, also, all ye sinners, for I announce to each and all of you that I, Jesus Christ, the true Son of God and of the Virgin Mary, your Creator, your Redeemer, your sovereign Lord, am about to exercise my office of Judge.

"With infinite patience I have borne with your innumerable iniquities: the time of grace is now past, the time of justice has come. Every one shall be rewarded according to his works. Those who have done good shall presently go with Me into eternal life, and those who have done evil shall be cast into the abyss of everlasting torment and anguish. All creation shall see and acknowledge that I am a just God, that I judge not according to appearances, but according to the measure of that which each man has deserved."

Some such words as these will proceed out of the mouth of the Judge, and they will be pronounced with such majesty that all men will quake and tremble. All miserable sinners will begin to weep and wail afresh, so that the very earth might be moved with compassion. "Alas for us poor wretches," they will exclaim with one voice, "how can we stand before the face of our Judge! Mountains, fall on us, and rocks, cover us, and hide us from the face of Him that sitteth upon the throne, and from the wrath of the Lamb. For the great day of their wrath is come, and who shall be able to stand?"

And since at every tribunal an accuser must be present, to bring charges against the individual who is to be judged, so at this general judgment the Angels and the devils will be the accusers of man kind. St. Michael will first stand forth and say: "Most just Judge, I bring an accusation against these millions of sinners, who defiled the earth to such an extent by their misdeeds, that Thou in Thy holy indignation didst see fit to purify it by fire; I call upon Thee now to punish these transgressors according to Thy justice."

Then Lucifer, speaking in the name of all the evil spirits, will raise his voice with a roar like that of a lion, and accuse all mankind in a body: "Most just Judge of the living and the dead, I bring a charge against all the human beings assembled here. Since it seemed right to Thy stern justice to banish me and all the Angels who joined with me from Heaven on account of one single sin, and to condemn us to everlasting damnation, it is only fair that Thou shouldst include all mankind in the same condemnation with myself, and cast all men here present into the abyss of Hell. For there is not one single individual here who has not committed sin, and trangressed Thy law."

Then Christ will answer the accusation in this wise: "It shall be done as you request, O ye Angels and ye demons; all men must appear before My judgment–seat, and each one shall receive that which is his due : chastisement to the wicked, recompense to the good."

When all those whom Christ has chosen to share with Him His office of Judge shall have taken their seats, His apostles having the precedence of all others, the judgment will commence. It appears from what the Apostle St. Paul says that no person, not even the Saints, will be exempted from this ordeal. "We shall all stand before the judgment– seat of Christ" (Rom. xiv. 10).

This standing before the judgment–seat of Christ will fill every one with fear. No one will be free from it; even the just will feel it to a certain degree, as well as the unhappy sinner. Even though the just may not be conscious of any sin, they will yet not be without apprehension. St. Paul says this, speaking of himself: "I am not conscious to myself of anything, yet am I not hereby justified, but He that judgeth me is the Lord" (i Cor. iv. 4). By this the Apostle apparently intends to say: "My conscience does not indeed reproach me, but this does not prove me to be one of the just; I must wait and see what sentence the eternal Judge will pass on me." In fact every man will be so terrified at the first sight of the irate Judge, that, like St. John, he will fall at His feet as dead.

It appears to me that judgment will be passed upon the good somewhat after this manner: The guardian Angels will lead those who have been committed to their charge to the judgment–seat of God, and then the just will fall before Him in lowly adoration. The evil enemy will then begin to accuse them, and bring forward everything that he can against them. But the guardian Angel will defend his client, he will produce all his good works, his penances, his virtues, and lay them in the scales of Divine justice. And if they are not too light, Christ will array him in the new robe, the garment of splendour, and crown him with the diadem of the eternal kingdom. Who can tell what the glory of that moment will be! How all the just will rejoice that their lot is among the blessed ! How kindly the choir of Angels will congratulate them, and exult with them in blissful jubilation. And how all who are yet waiting for their sentence will marvel at the glory that is theirs, and long to share it with them.

Most bountiful Jesus, in the name of all the Saints and elect, whom Thou dost destine to the enjoyment of eternal felicity, I beseech Thee of Thine infinite loving kindness, that I may stand amongst Thy Saints in the Day of Judgment. I am indeed unworthy of this favour, but for the greater honour and praise that will be ascribed to Thee, I pray Thee let Thy boundless mercy be manifested towards me; cast me not away, poor sinner that I am.

And I entreat you, Saints of God, to help me to attain to your blessed company. I know that your intercession is powerful enough with God to induce Him to look upon me with compassion, and be infinitely merciful to me in His judgment of my life. Amen.

X. On the Length of Time that the Final Judgment will Last

HOW long will the duration of the Last Judgment be? No definite answer can be given to this question, for it is a matter which no one knows; yet it may be conjectured that it will occupy a considerable period. Some indeed say that it will be over quickly, because God could judge all mankind in a single instant. Yet this opinion does not seem to be held by the Fathers of the Church, nor is it supported by Holy Scripture, in which we find a day of judgment invariably spoken of.

St. Paul, for instance, says: "God hath appointed a day wherein He will judge the world in equity" (Acts xvii. 31). And we read in the prophecies of Isaias: "Behold the day of the Lord shall come, a cruel day and full of indignation and of wrath and fury" (Is. xiii. 9). In these and many other passages of Holy Writ the Last Day is spoken of as a day, not an instantaneous judgment. The prophet Joel indicates that the day will be a long one, when he says: "The day of the Lord is great and very terrible; and who can stand it?" (Joel ii. 1 1.) And of this same day St. John, the prophet of the New Dispensation, also says: "The great day of their wrath is come, and who shall be able to stand it?" (Apoc. vi. 17.)

In many other passages of Holy Scripture we find similar expressions; the Day of Judgment being called a great day, which probably means a long day. St. Jerome held this opinion, for he says: "The day of the Lord will be a great day because of the eternity following upon it." St. Augustine, when speaking of the duration of the final judgment, expresses himself thus: "Over how many days the judgment will extend we have no means of ascertaining; yet we know that a considerable period is often designated in Holy Scripture as a day." St.

Thomas Aquinas agrees with St. Augustine on this point; he brings forward several arguments to prove that the final judgment will be of long duration.

And wherefore should God shorten that day? There is abundant reason why He should rather prolong it. For it is the day of Christ's greatest triumph; the day whereon the Saints attain their greatest glory and the damned are put to the greatest shame.

It is the day of Christ s greatest triumph, because He will not only be adored by all the Angels and Saints, but also by the wicked spirits and lost souls, and acknowledged by all to be their Judge. On that day all His enemies will be beneath His feet ; on that day all His foes will be forced to confess their offences against Him, the Divine Arbiter. They will then and there be compelled to own His divinity, His infinite charity, the countless benefits He has bestowed on them, in return for which they persecuted Him, blasphemed Him, put Him to a cruel death. Secondly, the blessed Saints will on that day attain their greatest glory, because they will be held in honour and esteem by all mankind, as well as by God and by the Angels. For Christ will then make manifest to all present how faithfully they served Him, with what self–sacrificing zeal they laboured for the conversion of sinners. He will then make manifest the secret penances they performed, the fierce temptations they resisted. He will then make manifest the pitiless persecutions they endured from the children of this world, and how all manner of evil was spoken against them unjustly. Thus Christ will crown them with the honour that is their due, and all their adversaries will be confounded.

Thirdly, on that day the reprobate will be put to the greatest ignominy and anguish. For the Judge will reveal all the shameful, the abominable character of their misdeeds: He will reveal in the sight of Angels and Saints, of the devils and the damned, the infamous deeds they performed under cover of darkness. Yes, He will pour out the full chalice of His indignation upon those wretched beings, who under the mask of their hypocrisy dared to desecrate His very sanctuary. He will cause those who have been corrupters of innocence to be seized and placed among the evil spirits, whose diabolical, thrice accursed work they carried on earth.

On that day the Divine Judge will give all the impenitent sinners to drink deeply of the cup of shame and ignominy, as St. Basil tells us, when he says: "The confusion that will overtake the godless sinner in the Day of Judgment will be more cruel torture to him than if he were cast into a flaming fire." This is in fact the reason why God has appointed the final judgment, that sinners may not only be punished by the pain which will be their portion, but that they may also be put to public shame. St. Thomas Aquinas says: "The sinner does not only deserve pain, he deserves disgrace and ignominy, for this is a punishment to which human beings only can be subjected. The lower animals can be chastised and put to death, but they cannot know what it is to suffer shame and contempt." This accounts for the fact that any one who has a single spark of self–respect would rather suffer the heaviest punishment in secret, than be exposed to public disgrace.

On all these grounds it will be surmised that the final judgment will stretch over a considerable period of time, and hence we have all the more reason to tremble at the prospect of it, and earnestly pray God that on that great day He will not overwhelm us with shame and confusion, but will grant us a share in His joy and glory.

XI. On the Publication of the Sentence Passed upon the Good and the Bad

WHAT has hitherto been said concerning the Last Judgment is indeed most awful, but that which is now to come is yet more so: we are about to speak of the sentence pronounced upon the wicked, and how they will be cast down into Hell. This is so terrible that nothing in all eternity can be found equal to it in horror.

When the supreme Judge shall have searched the hearts of all men, and weighed all their actions in the balance of justice, when all has been made open and manifest to the whole world, He will pass sentence upon the good and upon the bad. He will first turn a kindly countenance to His elect (who stand on the right hand), and address to them the consoling words: "Come, ye blessed of My Father, possess you the kingdom prepared for you from the foundation of the world. For I was hungry and you gave Me to eat; I was thirsty, and you gave Me to drink; I was a stranger and you took Me in, naked and you covered Me, sick and you visited Me; I was in prison and you came to Me" (Matt. xxv. 34–36).

You have been faithful to Me unto your life s end. You despised the world and all the things of the world, you loved Me and sought above all else to promote My glory. You suffered much whilst upon earth, you performed hard works of penance, you were despised and oppressed by the votaries of the world and by the wicked. But now the time of suffering is over and the time of happiness begins; your sorrow shall be turned into joy, eternal joy which no man can take from you.

"Therefore come, O My friends, come ye blessed and chosen of My heavenly Father, come from toil to rest, come from grief to joy, come from the realms of darkness to the regions of light, come from earth to Heaven. Come and possess the celestial country, for which you have longed so often, come and reign with Me forever, for by your good works you have merited this reward. Your felicity shall endure as long as I am God, and in My presence you shall enjoy the bliss of Heaven to all eternity." The hearts of the elect will overflow with joy and consolation and delight when they hear these propitious words. They will look up to the benign countenance of their Judge, and say to Him with joy and gratitude: "Most gracious God and Lord, Thy loving kindness towards us is infinite, and Thy bounty knows no bounds. How have we deserved to receive from Thee so rich a recompense?

What have we done to entitle us to endless felicity? It is of Thy mercy and infinite charity alone that Thou dost admit us to Thy kingdom of glory. Be Thou blessed for evermore; our mouth shall continually extol Thy majesty!"

After this, Christ will command His Angels to bring all the Saints before Him. And as they come up to His throne, He will array each one in a garment of glory, brilliant and beautiful, so that they will shine like stars. On their heads He will place golden crowns of surpassing brightness, and into their hands He will give lilies, roses, palm–branches, and a sceptre, to betoken the victory they have achieved over the world, the flesh, and the devil.

The lost will witness the glory and exaltation of the Saints. They will hear their shout of triumph and it will be to them gall and wormwood.They will gnash their teeth in rage and remorse; all the pleasure they felt in their sins will now be gone. They will mourn and lament, and say, amid sobs of deep despair: "Alas, how unfortunate, how miserable we are! What have we done ! Behold those whom once we despised now so happy, so enraptured, so honoured and glorified, and we, who thought scorn of them, are now so unhappy, so miserable, so disgraced, branded forever with every sign of reprobation! And yet we might have won for ourselves the same glorious destiny as they; the toil and difficulty would not have been beyond our strength. But we in our accursed folly have trifled away the supreme Good, and deprived ourselves of eternal felicity for the sake of worthless and transient pleasures. Oh, what folly, what madness on our part! How could we allow ourselves to be dazzled to such an extent by the vile debaucheries of the world!"

After these unhappy beings have bewailed their misery for a considerable time, the trumpet will again send forth a mighty sound. This blast of the trumpet is to announce the sentence passed upon the reprobate, and it will impose silence on every one present. Then the Judge will turn to the wicked, and, looking at them with a countenance kindled with holy wrath, He will say:

"O foolish, O blind sinners! Now the dreadful day has come whereof I spoke to you when I was upon earth the day, the hour of judgment." Now He stands before you whose enemy you have always shown yourselves. In your arrogant presumption you caused all manner of pain and injury to Me, to My Church, to My brethren and sisters, to all the children of God. Behold the wounds you inflicted on Me; behold the side which you pierced; behold the Cross whereon you nailed Me; behold the pillar at which you scourged Me, and to which in after years you bound My Church, my spotless spouse, for century after century, lacerating and tearing her flesh with the scourge of your insolent mockery, your unbelief, your scandals, your seductions, your infamous deeds of every sort.

" Out of love for you I came down from Heaven, and out of love for you I endured the cruelties of death. And yet My love, so wondrous in its extent, awakened no response in your hearts, met with no love in return ; on the contrary, you thrust Me away with contempt and hatred when I stood at the door of your heart as a suppliant, desirous of gaining admittance there. How often did I call to you, and you would not listen to Me. I stretched out my hands to you, but you drew back from My embrace. I employed threats, I visited you with many a loving chastisement, but you would not bow your proud neck beneath My sweet yoke. You deliberately chose to serve the devil as your god, and therefore you shall share his lot now, and be with him in the abyss of damnation to all eternity. I also will laugh at your destruction. Behold My servants, all the just, shall eat and be filled, whilst you shall hunger everlastingly. My servants shall be given to drink in abundance, whilst you shall thirst, and your thirst shall never be quenched. My servants shall rejoice and you shall mourn. My servants will exult in rapturous bliss, and you will shriek in agony and despair. Depart from Me, ye cursed, into everlasting fire which was prepared for the devil and his Angels. For I was hungry and you gave Me not to eat; I was thirsty and you gave Me not to drink; I was a stranger and you took Me not in, naked and you covered Me not, sick and in prison and you did not visit Me."

This verdict, pronounced by the just Judge, will strike the ears of the damned like a thunderclap; they will fall prostrate upon the ground, overwhelmed by these terrible words, and then they will raise such a cry of despair and rage, that the very Heavens and the earth will tremble at the sound.

"O woe betide us, accursed and miserable that we are ! We must now be banished from the presence of God and of the Saints to all eternity! We must burn forever and ever with the devils in the fires of Hell ! Depart into the everlasting fire! Oh, what an awful sentence from the lips of our Judge! Everlasting burning! Everlasting torment! No hope of rescue ! Woe betide us, wretched sinners; woe betide us, woe betide us!

Thus will the lost souls complain, and weep, and lament. Yet the time of grace is over; the sentence has been passed; there is no more mercy, no more clemency for them.

" Understand these things, you that forget God; lest He snatch you away and there be none to deliver you" (Ps. xlix. 22). Yes, understand this, O unhappy sinners, and see to it that a like doom does not overtake you. Think how you would feel, were you amongst the number of these reprobates. Consider what you would then wish that you had done, and what you would give as the price of your ransom, were it possible for you to be liberated.

Well, then, do now what you would then wish to have done. Confess and bewail your grievous sins whilst there is yet time, and pray God to preserve you from never–ending torment.

O most merciful God, Thou hast told us by the lips of Thy prophet: "In an acceptable time I will hear thee, and in the day of salvation I will help thee." Behold now is the day of salvation, wherefore I call upon Thee with the utmost confidence, and from the bottom of my heart I beseech Thee that Thou wouldst grant me grace and help in proportion to my necessities, that I may not finally be cast away. For the dead praise Thee not, O Lord neither those that go down into Hell, but the living, we who live in Thy presence, will extol Thy holy name forever and ever. Amen.

XII. How the Damned will ask in Vain for Mercy, and will be cast down into Hell

WE know from the testimony of Christ's own words that the damned will be permitted to speak to Him, after they have received their sentence. Then (that is, after the sentence has been pronounced) He tells us, "They also shall answer Him, saying: Lord, when did we ever see Thee hungry, or thirsty, or a stranger, or naked, or sick, or in prison, and did not minister unto Thee?" (Matt. xxv. 44.)

When the lost souls perceive that there is no remnant of hope that their terrible sentence of condemnation may be mitigated, they will, in their despair, pour out horrible imprecations: "cursed be the parents who gave us birth; cursed be all those who led us into sin; cursed be all men who have lived with us upon this earth; cursed be He Who created us; cursed be the blood of Christ, wherewith we were redeemed; cursed be all the Saints of God!"

What will the Divine Judge do when He hears them revile God in this shocking manner? When He Himself, standing before the Jewish council, acknowledged that He was the Son of God, the high priest Caiphas rent his garments and cried with a loud voice: "He hath blasphemed; now you have heard the blasphemy, what think you?"

And the people answering said: "He is worthy of death." The same scene will take place now, only it will be a thousandfold more terrible. When Christ hears these blasphemies He will exclaim, in holy indignation: "They have blasphemed God, they have cursed Me and My Saints! You have heard it yourselves, now what think you?"

Thereupon all the Angels and Saints will answer: "They are worthy of eternal death, of the everlasting pains of Hell! Away with them to the place of torment, away with them into everlasting fire!"

Then that will be fulfilled which is foretold in the book of Wisdom: "The Divine Judge will take zeal as His armour, and will arm the creature for the revenge of His enemies. He will put on justice as a breastplate, and will take true judgment instead of a helmet. He will take equity for an invincible shield, and He will sharpen His severe wrath for a spear, and the whole world shall fight with Him against the unwise. Then shafts of lightning shall go directly from the clouds, as from a bow well bent. They shall be shot out and shall fly to the mark. And thick hail shall be cast upon them from the stone–casting wrath; the waters of the sea shall rage against them, and the rivers shall run together in a terrible manner. A mighty wind shall stand up against them, and as a whirlwind shall divide them ; and their iniquity shall bring all the earth to a desert, and wickedness shall overthrow the thrones of the mighty" (Wisd. v. 18–24).

In these awful words Holy Scripture, the book of truth eternal, describes the sacred indignation wherewith the supreme Judge will chastise the damned whilst they are still upon the earth. All the elements, thunder, lightning, hailstorms, the raging billows of ocean, whirlwinds, and tempests, all the powers, in short, of nature will become instruments to execute the vengeance of God upon those who have rebelled against Him, against the abandoned wretches whose existence upon earth has been one long and terrible outrage against their Creator. For in their words and works they have blasphemed Him, the God of infinite holiness, power, and loving kindness. They have wantonly offended the Creator and Preserver of the realm of nature; therefore all nature rises up against them in vengeance.

Now, when Christ has poured out upon these unhappy beings all the rage of the powers of nature in their vindictive and primitive fury, the earth will open beneath their feet, and they, together with all the devils, shall be swallowed up.

St. John, in the Apocalypse, says: "And a mighty Angel took up a stone, as it were a great millstone, and cast it into the sea, saying: With such violence as this shall Babylon, that great city, be thrown down, and shall be found no more at all" (Apoc. xviii. 21).

Do not these words that the Angel uttered signify that all the lost souls will go down into Hell with the impetus of a millstone that sinks to the bottom of the abyss of waters into which it is hurled ?

O, awful fall of the damned! Who can think of it without shuddering! Alas for those for whom it is prepared; better were it for them that they had never been born!

Thus they will descend, and Hell, when they reach it, will, like a fierce dragon, open its jaws to devour them, and they will be engulfed within them, according to the prophecy of Isaias: "Hell hath enlarged her soul, and opened her mouth without any bounds, and then strong ones, and their people, and their high and glorious ones, shall go down into it" (Is. v. 14).

Who can portray the despair of the damned, the rage wherewith in the deep and sombre abyss of Hell they will seek in their fury to tear and lacerate one another. What words can describe the howls and groans that will re–echo through that place of torment ? It is beyond the power of man to conceive. For if Holy Scripture tells us that eye hath not seen, nor ear heard, neither hath it entered into the heart of man what God hath prepared for them that love Him, may it not also be said that man cannot form any idea of what God has prepared for those who have so frequently, so wantonly, insulted Him? And if the joys of Heaven surpass all our powers of description, will not the torments of Hell also be inconceivably great?

Reflect upon this, O reader, reflect upon it often, and do not fritter away thy life in idle pleasures, but look to it that thou save thy soul. Call upon God with all the fervour of thy heart, and beg Him to grant thee a favourable sentence in the day of final judgment, saying:

Most just God, and Judge of all men ! Many times, and grievously, I have offended Thee, and I have nought to expect from Thy justice but severe chastisement.

Yet I now confess my misdeeds; I repent of them and abhor them, and I firmly purpose from this time forth to be ever faithful unto Thee. Wherefore, I beseech Thee mercifully to pardon my sins, in order that I may escape eternal death, and may attain everlasting felicity. Amen

XIII. How the Blessed will go up into Heaven after the Judgment

WHEN the earth has opened and swallowed up the lost souls, then the Angels and the blessed will exult and rejoice. They will extol the justice of God, and confess that the reprobates fully deserved their fate.

St. John, in his Apocalypse, gives a beautiful description of how the blessed will rejoice and magnify the justice of God.

"I saw an Angel come down from Heaven, having great power ; and the earth was enlightened with his glory. And he cried out with a strong voice, saying: Babylon the great is fallen, is fallen: and is become the habitation of devils. For her sins have reached unto Heaven, and the Lord hath remembered her iniquities. Render to her as she also hath rendered to you, and double unto her according to her works. As much as she hath glorified herself, and lived in delicacies, so much torment and sorrow give ye to her. Rejoice over her, thou Heaven, and ye holy apostles and prophets, for God hath judged your judgment on her.

" After these things, I heard, as it were, the voice of much people in Heaven, saying: Alleluia! Salvation, and glory, and power, is to our God. For true and just are His judgments, who hath judged the great harlot which corrupted the earth with her fornication, and hath revenged the blood of His servants at her hands. And again they said : Alleluia ! And the four–and–twenty ancients fell down and adored God that sitteth upon the throne, saying, Amen! Alleluia! And a voice came out from the throne saying: Give praise to our God, all ye, His servants, and you that fear Him, little and great. Alleluia! For the Lord our God, the almighty, hath reigned. Let us be glad and rejoice, and give glory to Him, for the marriage of the Lamb is come, and His wife hath prepared herself.Blessed are they that are called to the marriage supper of the Lamb."

These words do, indeed, present a delightful prospect. How excellent will be the triumph–song of the Saints when they go in as guests to the marriage of the Lamb! How sweetly they will sing Alleluia ! How fervently they will thank God for having delivered them from eternal damnation, and numbered them amongst His elect!

The ascension into Heaven will next take place. Can one venture to describe this also ? The sweetest strains of music will fill the air. St. Michael will head the glorious procession, carrying the cross whereon Christ died. For the cross and all the other instruments of the Passion will be preserved in Heaven at least such is the opinion of several learned theologians.

Following upon these sacred relics will come the first choir of Angels, together with those members of the company of the saved, to whom the sentence of Christ has assigned a place in the lowest of the Angelic choirs. Children who have died in infancy, and souls who have persisted in sin unto the last, and yet have been saved through the infinite mercy of God and real contrition on their part, will be with the first choir of Angels. How fervently they will praise their God for His unspeakable compassion!

Next will come the choir of archAngels, and with them those Saints who have deserved a place in this second Angelic choir. God–fearing married people, devout widows, besides other pious persons who have lived in the world, will, adorned in marvellous beauty, laud and magnify God with the archAngels.

In the third place will come the choir of powers, amongst whom will be all priests who have led a holy life on earth.

The choir of the principalities will come next, with all the Saintly bishops and prelates who have ruled the Church to the glory of God and the salvation of those who have been subject to them.

The choir of virtues will come fifth with the doctors of the Church and all who, by their doctrine and preaching, have converted unbelievers, and brought them to the knowledge of the true faith.

In the sixth place will come the choir of the dominations, with the confessors who suffered great persecution for the faith, and died in misery and destitution for Christ s sake.

The choir of the thrones will follow next, with the holy martyrs who shed their blood, and gladly gave up their lives for the name of Christ.

The eighth choir is that of the cherubim, amongst whose ranks will be those holy virgins who have not merely kept their chastity unsullied, but who, consumed by Divine charity, have led a life of highest perfection.

The ninth and highest of the Angelic choirs is that of the seraphim. With them will be the holy apostles and servants of Christ, who, following in the footsteps of the Redeemer, have lived on earth an Angel s life.

In a word, every one of the blessed will have his place assigned him in whichever of the Angelic choirs for whose company his virtues render him most fit.

How glorious will be the procession of the choirs, and how melodious the celestial canticles they will sing ! Words fail us when we attempt to describe it.

And to close the triumphal cortege the King of Heaven and earth comes, crowned with splendour, Christ, the first begotten Son of the heavenly Father, accompanied by His most blessed Mother the Virgin Mary. He is surrounded with such beauty and majesty, that Heaven and earth, Angels and men, are struck with amazement. In fact this ascension into Heaven will be in every respect attended with such grandeur and glory, it will be so inexpressibly sublime and beautiful, that the lips even of an Angel would fail to give an adequate idea of it.

Consider what will be the rapture of the redeemed when they soar aloft through the air, both soul and body, as if they were pure spirits, ascending ever and ever higher, beyond the shining orbs of Heaven with their golden refulgence, approaching nearer and nearer to the heavenly Jerusalem, the city of God. And oh! what ecstatic joy will inebriate them when they enter through the golden gates, and be hold the splendour and magnificence of the city of God. When the Queen of Saba saw the magnificence of Solomon's palace, she was struck dumb with astonishment. But a greater than Solomon is there, and the majesty and loveliness of the palace of the King of kings is infinitely greater than that of any earthly monarch.

Hence we may surmise what the blissful rapture of the blessed will be, when it is granted them to behold what God has prepared for them that love Him.

Dost thou not desire, O pious Christian, to dwell with the redeemed and enjoy the unspeakable delights of the city of God, the heavenly Jerusalem? Assuredly thou dost desire it. We all of us have within us a powerful impulse, an ardent longing for happiness and enjoyment. O, seek not after that happiness, strive not to secure the enjoyment for which thy soul thirsts in this valley of tears. Lift up thine eyes to the land that is above, let that be thy goal, and one day thou shalt ascend up on high with jubilant songs. God grant to thee and to me, reader, that by His grace, this happy lot may be our portion.

PART III

ON HELL

I. On the Fire of Hell

ALTHOUGH in the present day many are found to deny the existence of Hell, or, at any rate, the eternity of punishment, we do not consider it incumbent upon us to bring forward a number of proofs that there is such a place as Hell. In the case of the Christian reader, for whom this book is intended, evidence of this nature is quite superfluous, because he will not have made shipwreck of his faith. Indeed, what further proofs can be required for the existence of Hell and the eternity of punishment, seeing that the prophets, that Christ Himself, that the apostles, and the Fathers of the Church, nay, the very Turks and heathens, speak of it as an unquestioned fact. Those who deny the existence of Hell must consequently be counted amongst the fools who say in their heart that there is no God who punishes their misdeeds.

It would undoubtedly be very agreeable for these people if all things ended with this life, if there were no day of reckoning, or if, at least, the infernal regions were somewhat less intolerable. This accounts for their catching at any apparent arguments wherewith to delude themselves and lull to sleep their fear of the eternal chastisements of Hell. We will not enter upon any examination of the wretched sophisms wherewith these fools deceive themselves ; for the teaching of the Catholic Church on this point is all we need* She teaches that there is a place or state of unequalled and never–ending pain in reserve for the damned.

We know that there really is fire in Hell, from the words Christ spoke to the wicked : " Depart from Me, ye cursed, into everlasting fire, which was prepared for the devil and his Angels " (Matt. xxv. 41). This shows that there is real fire in Hell, and that in it the damned must burn eternally. What the intensity of that pain will be it is beyond the power of man to depict. For of all the varied kinds of physical suffering to which man can be subjected, there is none so great, so cruel, so agonizing, as that which is caused by fire. The rack, the wheel, amputation of a man s limbs, are all terrible torture, but they are not to be compared to the pain of burning. If one does but touch a red–hot iron, what exquisite pain it occasions! In a moment the skin is off, the raw flesh protrudes, blood and matter exude from the wound, and the pain goes to the very marrow of our bones. One cannot refrain from crying out and screaming as if one had lost one's senses. Now if momentary contact with the red–hot iron causes such acute pain, what would it be if one had to hold a red–hot iron for any length of time !

Now just imagine that thou wert sentenced to be burned alive for thy sins, and for the whole of a live long day thou didst stand amid the flames, unable to die. How piteously thou wouldst weep and wail, how loudly thou wouldst shriek and roar in thy agony, so that the heart–rending cries wrung from thee by the torture thou endurest would not only cause the bystanders to shudder, but fill them with sincere compassion. That man must indeed be stony–hearted who could bear to look unmoved on such a spectacle.

Ere long thou wouldst be burned to such an extent as to be no longer recognizable, reduced to the semblance of a glowing cinder. Now consider, O Christian, if the action of earthly fire causes such intolerable agony, what will be the torture of Hell– fire, the heat of which is incomparably more intense and more searching than that of any fire where with we are familiar. And if thou dost ask why Hell–fire should so far exceed earthly fire in the intensity of its heat, there are several reasons which account for this fact.

In the first place, every one knows that the larger the fire, the greater the heat it throws out. The flame of a wax taper is not very hot, but if the whole taper is burning at once, the flame arising from it is much hotter. When a house is on fire, the heat in the immediate neighbourhood is very great, but if a whole village is in flames, the heat of the conflagration becomes unbearable even at a distance. If such be the effect produced by the fire of earth, which is comparatively but small in its extent, what will the action be of the fire of Hell, that is immeasurably greater than any conflagration seen upon earth!

Secondly, a fire that is enclosed in a furnace burns far more fiercely than if it were in the open air, because the heat being shut in cannot escape and diffuse itself, or be tempered by the surrounding air. If that is so, with what fury the flames of the huge furnace of Hell will rage, with what intensity they will glow! Suppose such a misfortune as a man being thrown into a lime–kiln, or a furnace heated to white heat how terrible would be his sufferings!

The next reason why the fire of Hell surpasses in intensity of heat all other fire is that it is kindled by the breath of God. For the prophet Isaias says:

"Behold, the wrath of the Lord burneth and is heavy to bear, His lips are filled with indignation, and His tongue as a devouring fire. His breath as a torrent overflowing even to the midst of the neck, to destroy the nations unto nothing." And again: " Topheth (Hell) is prepared from yesterday, deep and wide. The nourishment thereof is fire and much wood ; the breath of the Lord as a torrent of brimstone kindling it" (Is. xxx. 27, 33).

What a frightful description is here given of Hell and its torturing fire. Do not say that in these and other familiar passages of Holy Scripture the expressions employed are mere figures, whereby the prophets foretold the Divine judgments about to fall on sinful nations, and not to be taken in a literal sense, as referring to Hell and its punishments.

Let us not deceive ourselves. These images are,it is true, in their primary signification to be understood as indicating the doom of sinful nations, but, in a wider and a higher sense, according to the interpretation given of them by the exponents of Scripture, they are predictions of the judicial chastisement which, after the final judgment, will be the portion of reprobate sinners.

St. Bridget justly says in her revelations: "The heat of Hell–fire is so great that if the whole world were wrapped in flames, the heat of the conflagration would be as nothing in comparison with it."

Hence we learn that that earthly fire bears no more resemblance to the fire of Hell than the feeble flame of a wax taper to the white heat of a glowing furnace. Remember this, O sinner, and lay it well to heart. St. Augustine tells us that the most fearful fire on earth is, in comparison with the fire of Hell, like a painting of fire compared to a real fire.

When thou seest a fire, call to mind the fire of Hell. And since thou couldst not endure to put thy hand for a single instant into that fire, think what the heat of Hell–fire must be, surpassing as it does so infinitely the small fire thou seest before thee.If thou canst not bear this, how canst thou endure the other?

It has now been made clear that the damned will one day be cast, body and soul, into the huge and awful furnace of Hell, into the immense lake of fire, where they will be surrounded by flames. There will be fire below them, fire above them, fire all round about them. Every breath will be the scorching breath of a furnace. These infernal flames will penetrate every portion of the body, so that there will be no part or member, within or without, that is not steeped in fire.

How despairing the cries, how agonizing the shrieks that will ascend from this bed of torture! "Woe to us miserable creatures! Woe to us a thousand times! We are tortured in this flame! The excruciating pain pervades every member of our body; the intolerable agony leaves us no rest! If only we could die, if only we could die so as to escape this fearful torture! Alas, this wish is all in vain! Dead as far as the life of the soul is concerned, dead because we have forfeited the grace, the mercy of God, we are yet condemned to live on, to live forever and ever!

"What a privilege death, annihilation would be to us! But it eludes our grasp; we can no longer hope that it will come to deliver us from this misery, this torture, from the furnace of Hell. Alas, how great has our folly been ! For the worthless pleasures of a moment we have incurred this intolerable misery, a misery which will endure for all eternity."

"Understand these things," says David, "you that forget God, lest He snatch you away and there be none to deliver you." Listen to this, O sinner, and let the lamentations of the lost be instructive to thee. Picture to thyself the pit of fire in which these wretched creatures have to expiate their sins. Wouldst thou, we ask again, for any sum of money, however large, agree to spend a single day immersed in those flames? No, not for the whole world wouldst thou agree to remain in that fire for one short hour.

If this be so, why dost thou for the sake of some sinful enjoyment, some unjust gain, voluntarily cast thyself forever into Hell–fire? O what folly, what consummate folly! God grant that these blind sinners may be enlightened, in order that they may become aware of the unwisdom of their conduct, and may apply themselves in time to the things which concern their salvation.

O God of justice ! how great is Thy wrath and how all–powerful is Thy hatred of sin and of the sinner ! Woe betide me and all who have the terrible misfortune to commit mortal sin. May God keep me from such sin as would be the means of casting me into eternal perdition. I will gladly suffer all things, the greatest temporal troubles, the acutest pains, even the cruellest death, in order to escape everlasting torment in Hell. This is my firm purpose; wherefore grant me Thy grace and strengthen me in my good resolution.

Nihil Obstat: Thomas L Kinkead, Censor Liborium

II. On the Hunger and Thirst Suffered in Hell

JUST as the crimes whereby the sinner in this life provokes the anger of God are of various kinds, so the pains of Hell whereby those crimes will be punished also vary in their nature. We know that men often sin through intemperance, greedily indulging themselves in food and drink. Consequently God has appointed a severe penalty for this sin in the next world. Christ foretells it, indeed, in the words: "Woe to you that are filled, for you shall hunger" (Luke vi. 25).

When Our Lord utters the word "Woe," He always intends to threaten or predict some great calamity. Let us consider for a moment what it really is in this case. It is impossible for us to form a true idea of the pangs of hunger, because we have never felt them. If for a whole day one has nothing to eat, the time seems very long, and one wants some food very much. And if one were deprived of any nourishment for two or three days, what misery it would be! But if a man had nothing whatever to eat for a whole week, and were left a prey to hunger, what would become of him?

In times of dearth and famine one is horrified to see what are the effects produced by hunger, and what a terrible visitation the scarcity of food is. For to still the intolerable pangs of hunger people will devour whatever they can lay their hands on; grass, leaves, unclean and disgusting animals, nay, men have even been driven to feed on the flesh of their fellow–men, mothers to sacrificing their children, and some have been known to gnaw their own flesh. And when the poor famished wretches have nothing more, they wander about like shadows of their former selves, pale and emaciated as death itself.

They drag on a lingering existence, until all their strength is consumed; finally, through the torture of starvation, they lose their senses; they rave and cry and howl, and die the most miserable of deaths.

If such are the effects of hunger upon earth, what will the hunger be which shall be experienced in Hell?

If want of food for a few days only causes such torture, what will a continual, never–ending hunger be? Who can think without horror of the hunger suffered in Hell! Woe betide those who have to endure it. The prophet Isaias testifies to the existence of real, actual hunger in Hell, in this passage of Holy Scripture: God thus speaks by the mouth of the prophet: "Because I called and you did not answer, I spoke and you did not hear; behold, My servants shall eat and you shall be hungry; behold, My servants shall drink and you shall be thirsty.

My servants shall rejoice and you shall be confounded; My servants shall praise for joyfulness of heart and you shall cry for sorrow of heart, and shall howl for grief of spirit" (Is. Ixv. 12, 13, 14). Who can tell how awful will be this hunger in Hell? The Psalmist says of the enemies of God that they shall suffer hunger like dogs (Ps. Iviii. 7). The reprobate shall then be constantly tormented by the most ravenous hunger, by a hunger so great as to exceed beyond measure the hunger endured in times of famine, by a hunger which will torment them forever.

What have you done, O unhappy sinners! You have brought upon yourselves this everlasting pain. Had you but done penance in this life, you would not have become the prey of this eternal hunger. But you desired to eat and be filled in your lifetime, consequently you must now endure what Christ foretold would be your fate:

"Woe to you that are filled, for you shall hunger."

Let those especially lay this to heart who are accustomed wilfully to neglect the observance of the prescribed fasts, and to eat meat on abstinence days. For whosoever eats meat on the fasts of the Church without necessity and without being dispensed, commits a grievous sin. To do so is tantamount to defying the Church and voluntarily excluding one's self from her blessing. And he who persists in this sin, and does not heartily repent of it, cannot hope for eternal felicity. What could be more rash and foolish than for so despicable a satisfaction to expose one s self to the danger of eternal perdition!

O, hardened sinner, whither art thou going !Think of the unending hunger to be endured in Hell, and have pity on thine own soul!

Besides hunger the damned suffer the most burning thirst, which it is beyond the power of words to describe. Every one knows how terrible are the sufferings caused by thirst: they are simply unbearable.

Those who are plagued by thirst will drink from the most impure sources, and if nothing at all can be obtained to quench their thirst, a lingering and painful death is the result. The thirst suffered by lost souls is infinitely greater, more intense, more painful than any thirst experienced on earth, however great that may be. If a mortal man could feel it even for a brief period, he would faint away and die immediately.

There is never any rest or respite for the damned; they are driven from one torment to another unceasingly. This occasions thirst. But the heat of Hell–fire, wherein they burn day and night, forever and ever, is the principal cause of the intolerable thirst that consumes them. They are immersed in flames, and never do they obtain the refreshment of a draught of water. My God, how great their thirst must be! It is unbearable, and yet they must needs endure it. Listen to the piteous appeal of a lost soul earnestly imploring the boon of a single drop of water: "Father Abraham, have mercy on me, and send Lazarus that he may dip the tip of his finger in water to cool my tongue; for I am tormented in this flame" (Luke xvi. 24). "Most merciful God, I ask only for water; I crave only one drop of water to give momentary relief to my burning tongue. Thou wilt not refuse so moderate a request, Thou who art praised by all Thy creatures as goodness itself."

But this supplication is in vain. God turns a deaf ear to the voice of their entreaty. Not a single drop of water is given to mitigate their sufferings.

Is it possible, O my God, that Thou canst be so stern? Father of compassion, why wilt Thou not hear their prayer? Thy justice and Thy hatred of sin will not allow Thee to yield; they oblige Thee to punish sin eternally and in the most terrible manner.

But we are told that not only are the damned tormented with excessive hunger and thirst, they are also fed with flames and given to drink of the chalice of Divine wrath. "If any man shall adore the beast, he shall also drink of the wine of the wrath of God, which is mingled with pure wine in the cup of His wrath, and shall be tormented with fire and brimstone. And the smoke of their torments shall ascend up forever and ever" (Apoc. xiv. 10). In the book of Moses we also read: "Their wine is the gall of dragons, and the venom of asps, which is incurable" (Deut. xxxii. 33).

Reflect, O sinner, upon this indescribable agony. Fire and brimstone will be the food of the damned, their drink the wine of God s anger. What can exceed such torture? My God, how rigorous Thou art ! How severe are Thy chastisements!

Think, you sinners, who now drink to excess, think what is the wine prepared for you hereafter, think of the fearful thirst that will consume you to all eternity. If you cannot bear to be thirsty for one day, how will you bear the burning thirst from which you shall never obtain relief? Reflect upon this in your heart, and indulge no longer in your intemperance. Give up this vice, which will infallibly drag you down to perdition.

St. Paul expressly closes the door of Heaven against you, when he says: "Drunkards shall not possess the kingdom of God" (i Cor. vi. 10).

There you have your sentence, pronounced upon you beforehand. If you continue to pursue your evil way, you cannot plead ignorance as to where it will finally condemn you.

III. On the Vile Odors of Hell

IN order that nothing may be wanting to the plagues of Hell, wherewith the lost souls are tormented, God has in His anger decreed that this horrible prison should be pervaded by an abominable stench, as a punishment for those who, when on earth, have taken excessive delight in the use of choice perfumes.

The prophecy of Isaias will thus be fulfilled: "Instead of a sweet smell there shall be a stench" (Is. iii. 24). Decaying animal matter emits so horrible an odour that no one likes to go near it. But if we imagine not one tainted carcass, but hundreds of thousands heaped together, the air for miles round would be so infected that it would cause the death of all in the vicinity.

Even this stench, however, when compared with the stench of Hell, seems as nothing, or rather as a pleasant odour. The effluvium of Hell arises primarily from the place itself, which is by its nature a most horrible and foul region. No breath of pure air can ever penetrate the closely–shut walls of that prison. Moreover, the whole of Hell is a lake of burning brimstone and pitch, and every one knows how offensive are the fumes they give out.

"The unbelieving, and the abominable, and murderers, and whoremongers, and sorcerers, and idolaters, and all liars shall have their portion in the pool burning with fire and brimstone, which is the second death" (Apoc. xxi. 8.)

The prophet of the New Dispensation here speaks of a pool, full of stagnant, foul, stinking water, for which there is no outlet. He adds that this pool is filled with burning brimstone from which a dense smoke ascends, as he says elsewhere: "The smoke of their torments shall ascend up forever and ever."

The very bodies of the reprobate are so foul and disgusting that they emit a most offensive odour, worse than any stench in this world. According to St. Bonaventure, the body of a single reprobate would so taint the air on earth as to cause the death of all living beings coming near it.

If one single body emits so horrible a stench, what can the exhalation be that rises from many millions of these wretched beings?

It is related of the tyrant Maxentius that he was wont, as a punishment, to cause a living man to be bound to a corpse, face to face and limb to limb, until the unhappy victim fainted, or even died through contact with the dead and decomposing body. That is indeed a torture of which no one can think without shuddering. How much worse will it be in Hell, where the bodies will lie close to one another, without any hope of being separated.

Bad as this stench is, it is greatly increased by the presence of the devils, who naturally are far more offensive to the nostrils than the bodies of the lost.

We read in the life of St. Martin that the evil one appeared to him upon one occasion, and the stench that filled the room was so overwhelming that the Saint said to himself: "If one single devil has so disgusting an odour, what can the stench be in Hell, where there are thousands of devils all together?"

How much suffering this abominable stench must cause to the damned ! how it must aggravate their distress and pain ! For it must be pestilential beyond description, arising as it does from so many different sources Hell itself, the bodies of the damned, the devils, the worms and reptiles, the fire of pitch and brimstone, each and all of which stink in the nostrils of the lost. Judge by what has been said how insupportable the combined odours of all these things must be.

Alas for the unfortunate beings who are condemned to breathe such an atmosphere! Alas for the poor sinners who have to dwell in it for endless ages! They must sink under it, they must constantly be on the verge of death. O my

God, I beseech Thee by Thy infinite clemency, spare me from so terrible a fate.

IV. Some Other Torments of Hell

IT is the opinion of many that some of the reprobates will be doomed among many other intolerable pains, to endure a most fearfully intense cold.

The venerable Bede relates the following anecdote of a man whose name was Trithelmus. This man was dangerously sick, and one night he was thought to be dead. The next morning he recovered consciousness, to the astonishment of all who were with him, and rose from his sick bed, saying that God had granted him a prolongation of days, in order that he might lead a different life to that which he had hitherto led.

After dividing his property amongst his children, and giving a portion of it to the poor, he entered upon an excessively different mode of life. Shutting himself up in a small tent beside a river, he spent his days and nights in weeping. In winter time he plunged up to the throat into the icy waters of the river, and then, shivering and benumbed by the cold, he immersed himself in hot water, a proceeding which caused him such agony that he could not restrain his cries.

When questioned as to the reason of his strange conduct, and how he could possibly bear the sudden alternations of extreme heat and extreme cold, he replied: "I have seen worse things than that." "What didst thou see?" the others asked him.And he replied: "I have seen how the unhappy souls in another world are cast out of a raging fire into icy cold, and from icy cold back into the burning flames. When I realize what they have to endure, I count my slight sufferings as nothing."

This anecdote, related by so grave and holy a man as venerable Bede, shows how terrible indeed are the torments of Hell.

Christ speaks to us of the darkness of Hell in these solemn words: "Bind his hands and feet and cast him into the exterior darkness: there shall be weeping and gnashing of teeth" (Matt. xxii. 13). Our Lord speaks of the darkness of Hell as exterior darkness, the most appalling, the most fearful that can be. A traveller who has lost his way in a forest and is benighted, feels a nameless terror coming over him.

Now there is a land which is covered with the shadow of death, where no order, but an eternal horror reigns. That land is Hell. An oppressive gloom weighs upon the lost; an indescribably terrible darkness prevails.

In this world sick people dread nothing more than the night, because the time seems to pass so slowly to them, and their pain seems doubly wearisome. They count the hours, and each one appears as long as the night. What will it be for the denizens of Hell, where thick darkness holds sway, and night never gives place to daylight?

In this horrible darkness the damned lie helpless as blind men, or as those who have had their eyes cruelly put out. They see nothing, for the acrid smoke stings their eyes, and the poisonous fumes of sulphur destroy their sight. We know how dense this smoke is from the account given by St. John: "To him (Satan) was given the key of the bottomless pit (Hell). And he opened the bottomless pit; and the smoke of the pit arose as the smoke of a great furnace; and the sun and the air were darkened with the smoke of the pit" (Apoc. ix. 2). And again: "They shall be tormented with fire and brimstone, and the smoke of their torments shall ascend up forever and ever; neither have they rest day or night" (Apoc. xiv. u.)

These are indeed terrible threats, and this prophecy foretells in the plainest terms what will be the fate of those who are servants of sin and of the devil. They shall be tormented with fire and brimstone to such a degree that the smoke of their torment shall ascend forever and ever. O fearful words! O torture inexpressible!

Consider, O misguided sinner, what thy feelings would be if thou wert confined for one single day in this dark and noisome dungeon. Thou knowest how disagreeable pungent smoke is to the eyes and nostrils ; in fact, no one can remain in it for a quarter of an hour without being asphyxiated and half blinded. If this is so on earth, what will it be in Hell?

The existence of the damned is more like death than life; it is a living death, an everlasting, unlimited torture and misery. And since we are told that the smoke of their torment goes up forever, it follows of necessity that complete darkness must prevail in Hell. In connection with this subject, venerable Bede relates the experiences of the man Trithelmus (of whom mention has already been made) whilst he lay in a trance, and was supposed to be dead. On recovering consciousness, amongst other things he narrated the following: "I was conducted by a being clothed in shining garments through a country quite unknown to me, until we came to a region enveloped in thick darkness, that made me shudder with fear and horror. I could distinguish nothing but the figure of my guide. As we penetrated deeper and deeper into this obscurity, I perceived in the midst of the darkness an abyss of immense extent filled with smoke and a lurid glare, the sight of which caused my hair to stand on end with terror. From this abyss proceeded piteous wailing, which sounded as if a number of men and women were being put to cruel torture and death.

"But the worst was that my guide vanished, leaving me alone in this terrible spot. I cannot describe the agonized apprehension that took possession of me; in vain I looked around in the hope of finding succour or solace. The terror I felt was so great that I thought I should have died.

"When I looked down into the black abyss, I was afraid lest I should fall into it, and be lost, body and soul. For with the lurid flames that rose not of the abyss there came burning sparks that fell back into it with a deafening noise, besides masses of sulphurous smoke –like clouds that seemed as if they might at any moment sweep me down with them into the depths of the fiery gulf. These were all lost souls which were driven upwards like sparks from burning logs by the force of the underground fire.

"God alone knows what I suffered; a cold sweat broke out all over me. Whilst I stood there in this agony, not knowing which way to turn, there sounded from far above my head peals of laughter, and mingled with the laughter bitter weeping and howling. As this noise came nearer, I saw a number of devils who had with them five helpless souls whom they were persecuting and tormenting. The devils were in exultation, mocking and laughing; the souls were in despair, uttering lamentations and cries of poignant anguish. Imagine what my feelings were when I heard their cries, and observed that the accursed devils were coming nearer and nearer.

When they came close up to me, I was so over powered with terror that I thought I should have fainted, and I believe if God had not strengthened me, I should have died there and then.

"For the demons glared at me with their fiery eyes in so alarming a fashion, and the poor souls called on me so pitifully for help, that I was divided between fear and compassion, and my heart was as if it must break. When the souls had been driven past me, they were precipitated into the depths of the abyss by the evil spirits with such violence that Heaven and earth seemed to tremble, and such a cloud of sparks flew upwards that I was afraid they would cover me. Finally, to my great grief and alarm, a number of evil spirits approached me, breathing rage and fury, and making as if they would drag me down with them into the black abyss.

"Then in abject terror I wept and wailed and implored help from some quarter; for in this dense darkness I beheld nothing but mocking devils, the yawning gulf and leaping flames, and knew not whither to turn for deliverance.

"When my distress was at its height, my guide reappeared; he rescued me from my enemies, and conducted me out of that dark, foul, horrible place. He told me moreover that I was to return to my body, and that I was to make known to as many as possible of my fellow–men, the existence of this land of terrible darkness."

In addition to the sinister obscurity that prevails in Hell, caused by the stifling smoke that rises in dense clouds from the lake of brimstone, there is the presence of frightful demons who increase the pain and torment of the damned.

We read in the legend of St. Anthony the Hermit, that the demons frequently appeared to him under various forms, plaguing and frightening him in indescribable ways. Sometimes they took the shape of wild beasts, lions, bears, dragons or savage dogs; at other times they appeared in human form, that of fierce–looking men, beautiful women, or monsters of hideous aspect. Sometimes they beat and maltreated him so barbarously that they left him half dead; sometimes they caused him such terror by their strange spectral apparitions, that had not God and his Angel guardian come to his aid, he would have incontinently expired.

Now if they did all this to a man of Saintly life, over whom they had no rightful power, what will they not do in Hell to the ungodly sinners who are completely at their mercy?

Doubtless these diabolical spectres, assuming the shape of wild animals, will fall upon the wretched sinners and mishandle them shamefully. This will be a fresh misery for them. No one can imagine what new terrors and torments the ingenuity of these spirits of Hell will devise to harass the damned and pour out on them their devilish malice.

If thou dost fear this darkness, and all the horrors attending it, see that thou fear the works of darkness, whereof Christ says: "Every one that doeth evil hateth the light, and cometh not to the light, that his works may not be reproved" (John iii. 20).

But if thou lovest darkness, and seekest the dark ness that thou mayst sin with greater impunity, it will be no act of injustice on God s part to cast thee into everlasting darkness, and at thy death to say to the devils: " Because throughout his life he has loved darkness and the works of darkness, bind his hands and his feet and cast him into the exterior darkness, where shall be weeping and gnashing of teeth."

Would that all obdurate sinners could see this, and consider the frightful torments which await the careless and indifferent. For in that wherein we have sinned we shall also be punished. And as in our own day there are so many tepid and negligent Christians who have not the slightest zeal for religion or religious exercises, we bid them beware lest they be one day cast into Hell–fire at the command of Him who calls Himself a jealous God, and who is alone to be feared because He can " destroy both body and soul into Hell."

Wherefore consider, O cold and careless Christians, what a fate is before you. Truly, were you to reflect upon these frightful torments, you would at once enter upon a new life. Instead of being tepid, sluggish, lax, cold Christians, you would quickly become zealous, active, scrupulous, fervent servants of God.

Away, then, with all tepidity, all indifference in the great business of our salvation. Whosoever thou art who readest this, resolve to fulfil thy duties as a Christian with all earnestness. Approach the sacraments more frequently than thou hast done hitherto; hear Mass more frequently than hitherto, be more instant and fervent in prayer than hitherto. Think more often of God and of the last things. Thus thou wilt surmount the indifference, the coldness that has crept over thee, thou wilt make God thy friend, the hope of eternal felicity will rise up within thee and become a blessed certainty. God grant that by His grace it may be so with thee and with me!

V. On the Company of Hell

THERE are many bold sinners who, when they are punished for their crimes and threatened with Hell–fire are wont audaciously to answer: "Wherever I go, I shall at any rate not lack company," as if the presence of others could afford any solace to them, or any alleviation of their torment. In order that these shameless sinners may see how wrong they are to speak thus, and how little cause they have to anticipate any relief from the company in which they will find themselves, this chapter shall be devoted to showing them how woeful that company will be, and how it will aggravate their misery.

The society of the damned consists of devils and lost souls. Both of these are countless in number. As for the society of the devils, this is so detestable that it may be reckoned as the worst penalty of the lost in Hell. The place of torment would be far less deserving of this name were there no devils in it. On account of the multitude of demons there, such confusion, such grief, such misery, such tyranny prevails, that it is heartbreaking even to think of it.

We mortals have no worse enemy than the devil, who hates us with so intense a hatred that he longs every moment to hurl us down into the abyss of perdition. And when at length he has got some one into his power, he deals with him more barbarously than savage despot ever dealt with his deadliest foe.

All the envy and hatred which at the time of his fall he conceived against God, and which he cannot vent upon Him, he vents upon the damned, tormenting them with plagues the very thought of which makes a man s blood run cold. Even if he were not to do any harm to the damned, the mere fact of his dwelling with them for all eternity would be such terrible misery for the unhappy sinners, that the horror of their position would be like a continual death to them.

Of all the fallen spirits, not one is so abominable as the chief of all, the haughty Lucifer, whose cruelty, malice and spite render him an object of dread not merely to the damned, but also to the devils subject to him. This Lucifer is called by various names in Holy Scriptures, all indicating his malignity. On account of his repulsiveness he is called a dragon; on account of his ferocity, a lion; on account of his malice, the old serpent; on account of his deceitfulness, the father of lies; on account of his haughtiness, king over all the children of pride; and on account of his great power and might, the prince of this world.

Listen to what the Fathers of the Church and some expositors of Holy Scriptures say of the dreadful appearance that Satan presents: they apply to him the description given of the leviathan in the book of Job: "Who can discover the face of his garment, or who can go into the midst of his mouth? Who can open the doors of his face? his teeth are terrible round about. His body is like molten shields, shut up close with scales pressing one upon another. One is joined to another, and not so much as any air can come between them. His sneezing is like the shining of fire, and his eyes like the eyelids of the morning. Out of his mouth go forth lamps, like torches of lighted fire. Out of his nostrils goeth smoke, like that of a pot heated and boiling. His breath kindleth coals, and a flame cometh forth out of his mouth.

In his neck strength shall dwell, and want goeth before his face. His heart shall be as hard as a stone, and as firm as a smith's anvil. When he shall raise him up, the Angels shall fear and, being affrighted, turn to God for protection. He shall make the deep sea to boil as a pot; there is no power upon earth that can be compared with him who was made to fear no one. He beholdeth every high thing ; he is king over all the children of pride" (Job xli.).

It is the opinion of St. Cyril, St. Athanasius, St. Gregory and other learned expositors of both the Greek and Latin Churches, that although this description, taken literally, is that of a monster of the sea, yet it is intended, in its mystic sense, to apply to Lucifer. And if one compares what is said of the leviathan with the attributes ascribed to the prince of darkness, it is impossible to deny their coincidence; moreover, one knows as a general fact that evil things have their types and figures in the natural world as well as good things, the one serving us for warning, the others for an example.

Besides the prince of darkness there are hundreds of thousands of inferior devils, which though less bad and abominable than himself, are yet so wicked and horrible that one could hardly look upon them and live.

St. Antony relates that one of the Brothers of his Order uttered a piercing scream at the sight of a devil who appeared to him. His fellow–monks, running to him in alarm, found him more dead than alive. After giving him something to revive and strengthen him, they asked him what was the matter. Then he told them that the devil had appeared to him, and terrified him so that all the life had gone out of him. And on their inquiring what the devil looked like, he answered: "That I really cannot say; I can only say that if the choice were given me I would rather be put into a red–hot furnace, than look again at the countenance of the demon."

We read much the same thing in the life of St. Catharine of Sienna. She too declared that she had rather walk through a flaming fire than gaze for one instant at the devil.

If the mere sight of the evil one is so appalling that the Saints think it more intolerable than the pain of exposure to a burning fire, what, my God, must be the fear and horror of the damned, dwelling forever in the midst of countless fiends!

How terrified thou wouldst be if a mad dog were suddenly to spring upon thee, pull thee to the ground, and begin to tear thee with his teeth ! Do not imagine that the devil will fall upon the damned with less fury, or treat them more mercifully. The account Job gives of his persecutors describes very accurately the state of a lost soul in Hell:

"My enemy hath gathered together his fury against me, and threatening me he hath gnashed with his teeth upon me; he hath beheld me with terrible eyes. They have opened their mouth upon me and reproaching me they have struck me on the cheek, they are filled with my pains. He hath taken me by my neck, he hath broken me, and hath set me up to be his mark. He hath compassed me round about with his lances, he hath wounded my loins, he hath not spared. He hath torn me with wound upon wound, he hath rushed in upon me like a giant" (Job xvi. 10–15). This passage will give us some idea of the awful character of the company the damned will find themselves among in Hell.

The reprobate may nevertheless perhaps console themselves with the thought: at any rate we shall have our fellow–men with us in Hell, and no lack of them either. Beware how you delude yourselves with this false comfort. Every lost soul would far rather be alone in Hell, were the option given him.

For as in Hell there is no Divine charity, so there is no love of one s neighbour; on the contrary, all the damned are so embittered one against the other, that they only wish evil to one another, and mutually mock at and curse one another in the most unkind manner.

And since on earth it is very grievous to be forced to live with an enemy who does one all manner of harm, so it is no small affliction to be continually with thousands of people, all of whom they hate and detest from the bottom of their heart.

What thinkest thou would be thy feelings if thou wast sorely tormented and maltreated and persecuted by devils, so that thou couldst not refrain from uttering loud cries of pain and vexation, and yet among all the thousands who bore thee company thou couldst not find one to show thee the slightest sympathy, but thou wert laughed at and cursed by all, for every one would rejoice in thy misery. Even thy father and mother, thy wife and children, thy brothers and sisters, thy friends and relatives would then be thy declared enemies, and instead of showing thee any gratitude would only seek to injure thee.

But amongst all thy enemies the most inveterate will be those to whom thou hast given scandal by thy bad example, whom thou hast led into sin by counsel or example, who owe to thee their perdition. They will hate and execrate thee so bitterly, and torment thee with such animosity that they will appear lesslike men than fiends incarnate.

In connection with this subject St. Bernardin relates the following instance: "A wealthy usurer had two sons, one of whom entered a religious Order, whilst the other remained in the world with his father. Not long after the father died, and in a short space of time he was followed to the grave by his son, to whom he had bequeathed all his property.

The other son, who had become a monk, was much concerned about the fate of his relatives, and earnestly implored almighty God to reveal to him their lot in another world. His entreaties at length prevailed; he was one day transported in spirit into Hell, but although he looked everywhere around him, he could not descry his father and his brother. Presently he noticed a fiery abyss, the flames of which rose up to a great height. In this pit of fire he saw those of whom he was in search, rivetted together with iron chains, raving and raging at one another. The father cursed his son, laying all the blame of his damnation upon him, saying: A curse upon thee, O wicked son, thou art alone the cause of my perdition. For thy sake, to make thee a rich man, I practised usury; had it not been for thee, I should not now be in this misery.Then the son retorted upon his father, saying: "A curse upon thee, O ungodly father, for thou art alone the cause of my perdition. Hadst thou not taken usury and bequeathed to me thy unjust gains, I should not have been the possessor of ill–gotten riches, and should not have come to this misery."

Thus will it be with thee, if thou art in any way responsible for the loss of a soul. Thy wife and children will anathematize thee, and reproach thee with the occasions of sin thou didst put in their way.

Dives felt this so keenly that he earnestly besought Father Abraham to send Lazarus to his father's house, to testify to his brethren of the sufferings he endured, lest they should also come to that place of torments. This he did not do out of love for his brothers, as St. Antony says, but because he was well aware that if they joined him in Hell, it would greatly aggravate his torment.

But supposing that natural affection still existed in Hell, especially between those who had sincerely loved one another on earth, and who had not been the cause of one another s damnation, the society of one who was dear to thee would augment rather than diminish thy pain, and this in proportion to the love thou hadst for him.

For what anguish it would be to thee to see thy dearest friend tortured and tormented in every possible manner. It would be enough to make your heart break asunder with sorrow and sympathy. And in addition to the mental pain and grief, the damned increase vastly one another's exterior and bodily sufferings. In the first place, because they lie pressed closely one upon another. Secondly, because they all emit so offensive and insupportable a stench. Thirdly, because they howl so piteously, and make Hell re–echo with their woeful lamentations.

Of this Christ speaks when He says: "There shall be weeping and gnashing of teeth." He repeats these words more than once, to give them greater force, and to impress upon our minds the magnitude of the torture endured by the lost.

The devils, too, will unite their howls to the shrieks of the damned, and raise such a clamour that Hell itself shall tremble.

The torment of the damned will be further aggravated by the frightful appearance of their bodies and the horror wherewith they inspire one another. For St. Anselm says: "Just as no stench can be compared to the stench of the damned, so nothing in this world can give an idea of their hideous appearance."

Thus as often as one lost soul looks at another, so often will he shudder with disgust and loathing and abhorrence. Were there no other torture but this in Hell, it would suffice to render its inmates most miserable.

Finally, the torment of Hell is greatly augmented by the eternal shame which will be its portion.

St. Thomas Aquinas tells us that the sins of each one will be as fully known to the others as if they could behold them with their bodily eyes.

Every one can imagine what anguish this must be. For what is so painful on earth as to be put to open shame?

To a man who has lost his good name life is not worth living ; it is only a burden to him. In former times, in some countries, it was customary to brand evil–doers, robbers, for instance, with a mark on the forehead or the shoulder. What ignominy for any one who had a spark of self–respect! Whenever anybody looked at him, he must have blushed crimson.

The devil will brand all the reprobate with the mark of shame on their foreheads, or on that part of the body wherewith they sinned, in order that all the shameful deeds they perpetrated in their life time may be made known. It is this everlasting disgrace which God foretells to the sinner by the mouth of His prophet: "I will bring an everlasting reproach upon you, and a perpetual shame which shall never be forgotten" (Jer. xxiii. 40). Let the damned do what they will, no effort on their part will ever avail to efface this mark, or to conceal it from their fellow–sufferers. Thus, as St. Ephrem says, this shame and infamy will be more insupportable than Hell–fire itself, because it will keep constantly before their remembrance the sins whereby they defiled themselves on earth.

Dionysius, the Carthusian, speaks of one of his religious brethren in England, who, after a trance that lasted three days, gave the following account, at the earnest request of the monks, of what he had seen: "I was conducted by my guide a long way until we came to a region of gloom and horror, where were a countless multitude of men and women, all suffering terrible torments. These were the persons who had sinned with their bodies; they were plagued by huge fiery monsters, who sprang upon them, and, despite their resistance, clasped them and hugged them with their paws till they shrieked with pain.

Amongst those who were tormented in this manner I saw a man whom I knew very well, and who had been much esteemed and respected in the world. Seeing me, he cried aloud in piteous tones: Alas, alas! woe is me that I sinned as I did in my lifetime, for now the pain I endure grows greater day by day. But the worst of all, what I feel most acutely, is the shame and disgrace to which my sins expose me, for all know them, and all despise me and mock at me on account of them."

Hence it will be seen that, immeasurable as are the torments of Hell, what the damned dread yet more than physical torments is to be an object of scorn and derision to their fellows on account of their sins. And thus their misery, far from being lessened by the company of others, is vastly increased by it. Wherefore think not to console thyself with the thought of the companions thou wilt find in Hell, for their society is only to be dreaded. And in order that thou mayst never be brought into such company, beware of associating in this world with any who may lead thee into sin and perhaps bring thee to perdition.

VI. On the Loss of the Beatific Vision of God

WE have already spoken of many and very terrible chastisements inflicted on the damned, but these are but a very insignificant portion of the whole. They are countless in number; and so great and awful that, as St. Augustine says, all the suffering of this world is as nothing when compared with the everlasting fire and torments of Hell.

Just as the Apostle Paul says: "Eye hath not seen, nor ear heard, neither hath it entered into the heart of man, what things God hath prepared for them that love Him," so it may be said: Eye hath not seen, nor ear heard, what punishments God hath prepared for those on whom His just judgments fall. And when we read the fearful chastisements wherewith God threatens to overwhelm, even in this world, the transgressors of His holy law, may we not feel sure that He will pour out all the fury of His anger upon those bold sinners who set at naught His warnings, and with fiendish malice, persist in their iniquity unto their life's end?

Remember what God said to the people of Israel: "A fire is kindled in My wrath, and shall burn even to the lowest Hell; and shall devour the earth with her increase, and shall burn the foundations of the mountains. I will heap evils upon the transgressors of My law, and will spend My arrows among them. They shall be consumed with famine, and birds shall devour them with a most bitter bite; I will send the teeth of beasts upon them, with the fury of serpents. Without the sword shall lay them waste, and terror within, both the young man and the virgin, the sucking child with the man in years" (Deut. xxxii. 22–25).

Holy Scripture contains many similar and equally appalling menaces. There is no doubt that in the next world, where justice, not mercy, will rule, God will chastise the insolent violators of His holy commandments with an unsparing hand. The punishments of eternity will be without number and without limit. The damned will be encompassed with trouble and sorrow, with agony and torments innumerable. St. Bernard says the pains of the damned are countless, no mortal tongue can enumerate them.

Yet of all these pains, that which gives the keenest anguish is being deprived of the vision of God. It will never be given to the damned to behold the Divine countenance. This pain will far outweigh all the other torments of which we have spoken.

It is impossible for mortal man to understand how this can be so great an affliction for the damned.

Yet such is the teaching of the Fathers ; they all maintain that there is nothing which the lost bewail so bitterly as being shut out forever from the vision of God. Whilst we live in this world, we think but little of the vision of God, and what it would be to us to be deprived of it eternally. This arises from the bluntness of our perception, which prevents us from comprehending the infinite beauty and goodness of God, and the delight experienced by those who behold Him face to face. But after death, when we are freed from the trammels of the body, our eyes will be opened, and we shall at least to some extent perceive that God is the supreme and infinite Good, and the enjoyment of Him our highest felicity.

And then such an eager desire will take possession of our soul to gaze upon and enjoy this supreme Good, that she will be irresistibly drawn to God, and will long with all her powers to contemplate His ineffable beauty. And if on account of her sins she is deprived of this beatific vision, it will cause her the most intense anguish. No grief, no torture known in this world can be in any wise likened to it.

St. Bonaventure bears witness to this, when he says: "The most terrible penalty of the damned is being shut out forever from the blissful and joyous contemplation of the Blessed Trinity." Again, St. John Chrysostom says: "I know many persons only fear Hell because of its pains, but I assert that the loss of the celestial glory is a source of more bitter pain than all the torments of Hell."

The evil one himself was made to acknowledge this, as we read in the legends of Blessed Jordan, at one time General of the Dominican Order. For when Jordan asked Satan, in the person of one who was possessed, what was the principal torment of Hell, he answered: "Being excluded from the presence of God." "Is God then so beautiful to look upon?" Jordan inquired. And on the devil replying that He was indeed most beautiful, he asked further: "How great is His beauty?" "Fool that thou art," was the rejoinder, "to put such a question to me! Dost thou not know that His beauty is beyond compare?" "Canst thou not suggest any similitude," Jordan continued, "which may give me to some extent at least an idea of the Divine beauty?" Then Satan said: "Imagine a crystal sphere a thousand times more brilliant than the sun, in which the loveliness of all the colors of the rainbow, the fragrance of every flower, the sweetness of every delicious flavour, the costliness of every precious stone, the kindliness of men and the attractiveness of all the Angels combined; fair and precious as this crystal would be, in comparison with the Divine beauty, it would be unsightly and impure."

"And pray," the good monk inquired, "what wouldst thou give to be admitted to the vision of God?" And the devil replied: "If there were a pillar reaching from earth to Heaven, beset with sharp points and nails and hooks, I would gladly consent to be dragged up and down that pillar from now until the Day of Judgment, if I could only be permitted to gaze on the Divine countenance for a few brief moments."

Hence we may gather how infinite is the beauty of the face of God, if even the spirit of evil would submit to such physical torture as he describes for the sake of enjoying for a few moments the sight of that gracious and majestic countenance. There is therefore no doubt that nothing is a source of such anguish to the devils and the damned as being deprived of the beatific vision of God.

Consequently, if God were to send an Angel to the portals of Hell, with this message to the wretched denizens of that place of torment: "The Almighty has in His mercy had compassion on you, and He is willing you should be released from one of the penalties you endure; which shall it be?" What thinkest thou would be the reply? They would all as one man exclaim: "O good Angel, pray God that if only of His bounty He would no longer deprive us of the sight of His countenance! "This is the one favour they would implore of God. Were it possible for them, in the midst of Hell–fire, to behold the Divine countenance, for the joy of it they would no longer heed the devouring flames. For the vision of God is so beauteous, so blissful, so full of rapture and infinite delight, that all the joys and attractions of earth cannot compare with it in the remotest degree.

In fact, all celestial happiness, how greatsoever it might be, would be turned to bitterness if the vision of God was wanting; and the redeemed would choose rather to be in Hell, if they could there enjoy that Beatific Vision, than be in Heaven without it. Just as the privilege of be holding the Divine countenance constitutes the chief felicity of the blessed, the one without which all others would be no happiness at all, so it is the chief misery of Hell, that the lost souls should for ever be excluded from it. On this subject St. John Chrysostom says:

"The torments of a thousand Hells are nothing in comparison to the anguish of being banished from everlasting bliss and the vision of God."

To realize, in some measure, how great this pain of loss is, we should bear in mind that we have been created by God to be forever happy. This love of happiness, this yearning for it, which every one of us feels in his heart, will never be destroyed, not even in Hell. During this life men, impelled by this desire and blinded by passion, seek happiness in riches, in honours, in sensual gratification. These vain images of happiness deceive us so long as our soul is united with our body. But after the soul has severed her connection with the body, all these false, fleeting pleasures disappear, and she becomes aware that God alone is the source of all happiness, and that she can find happiness solely in the possession of Him.

No longer deceived by false appearances, no longer blinded by passion, she perceives clearly the ineffable, ravishing beauty of God and His infinite perfections ; she sees His infinite power in creating the world, His infinite wisdom in governing it, His excessive love for her in be coming man, in dying for her, in giving Himself to her as the food of her soul in the Blessed Sacrament, in destining her to share His own happiness forever in Heaven. This knowledge of the grandeur, of the goodness and loveliness of God will remain deeply impressed on her for all eternity. She will also see the justice of the punishments which God inflicts forever in Hell upon all those who do not keep His commandments.

Then the reprobate soul, yearning after happiness, and feeling irresistibly drawn to God, who alone can make her happy, endeavours to rush to God with all the impetuosity of her nature, in order to behold Him, to enjoy Him, to be united to Him; but she finds herself repelled with infinite force from God, and hated by Him on account of her sins. Were all the riches, honours and pleasures of the world now offered to that soul, she would turn away from them, and would even curse them all, for she yearns for God alone, and can be happy only in God.

The reprobate soul in Hell, spurred on by frightful pains, looks about her for some alleviation, for some word of comfort; but not even a sympathizing look greets her, for she is surrounded by cruel devils and bitter enemies. Not meeting with any compassion where she is, she raises her eyes to Heaven, and beholds it so beautiful, so enchanting, so delightful, so full of true happiness. She remembers that she was created and destined to enjoy its bliss, and now, in the midst of her most excruciating pains, she longs for its pleasures with a still more indescribable yearning, and makes extraordinary efforts to go there, but she cannot leave her abode of torment.

No one in Heaven seems to take any notice of her.She sees the throne that God, in His goodness, had prepared for her, now occupied by someone else ! There is no longer any room for her in Heaven. She beholds there some of her relatives, of her companions and acquaintances; but they do not heed her. She beholds all the elect in Heaven full of joy and gladness. They do not even sympathize with her, but as the Psalmist sings, "the just will rejoice when he shall see the revenge" (Ps. Ivii. ii).

In vain the reprobate soul calls on the Saints, on the Blessed Virgin and on our Divine Saviour Himself. She feels drawn to God by an irresistible impulse, and understands that God alone can quench her thirst for enjoyment and make her happy. She longs to see and possess Him; she repeatedly endeavours to spring towards Him, but she feels herself repulsed by Him with invincible force; she beholds herself the object of Divine wrath, of the Divine anathema. She is aware that her case is hopeless, and that she shall never be admitted into the mansions of the blessed, or leave the abode of endless misery.

Despair seizes her; she utters the most fearful imprecations against God and the elect, against Heaven, against herself, her parents, her companions, against all creatures. All Hell resounds with her horrid blasphemies, and she becomes, in her ravings, an object of terror to all the other reprobates.

VII. The Worm that Dieth Not

OUR Divine Saviour says: "If thy hand scandalize thee, cut it off; it is better for thee to enter into life, maimed, than, having two hands, to go into Hell, into the fire that cannot be quenched, where their worm dieth not, and the fire is not extinguished. And if thy foot scandalize thee, cut it off; it is better for thee to enter lame into life, than, having two feet, to be cast into the Hell of unquenchable fire, where their worm dieth not, and the fire is not extinguished. And if thy eye scandalize thee, pluck it out; it is better for thee with one eye to enter the kingdom of God, than, having two eyes, to be cast into the Hell of fire, where their worm dieth not, and the fire is not extinguished" (Mark ix. 42–47).

By these words our blessed Redeemer wished to impress on our minds the necessity of avoiding the occasions of sin and of making even the most painful sacrifices to avoid sin and thus escape the endless pains of Hell. He, moreover, wished to en grave deeply in our minds the fact that two of the most fearful torments of Hell are its unquenchable fire and its never–dying worm. We have seen in a foregoing chapter in what consists the terrible fire of Hell. It now remains to us to examine in what consists "the worm that dieth not."

All the senses of the reprobate have each their peculiar punishment; their reason, or intellect, is punished by the pain of loss, as we have seen in the preceding chapter, a punishment far surpassing that of the senses. The memory of the reprobate is tormented by " the worm that dieth not," that is by a most keen and constant remorse of conscience, which will give them no rest.

The lost sinner will remember how many graces and means of salvation he had during life to save his soul ; how God sent him so many holy inspirations, how he received so many good instructions, how he had the grace of prayer within his power to enable him to practise the virtues of his state, to overcome temptation, to keep the Commandments of God and of His Church; how his pious friends exhorted him to lead a good life both by their exhortations, but especially by their good example; how he had so many opportunities of instructing himself in his obligations by the hearing of the word of God and the reading of good books, and of strengthening himself in the discharge of his duties by the reception of the Sacraments and by the practice of devotion to the Blessed Virgin!

The lost sinner will, in a word, remember with how little trouble he might have saved his soul and avoided Hell. He will say to himself: " So little effort was required for my salvation; even after my numerous sins a good confession would have sufficed. But through shame, through human respect, I did not make it. How foolish I was! How often did my conscience, my family, my friends urge me to go to confession! But it was all in vain. Others committed greater sins than I did, but they bewailed them, went to confession and changed their life, and now they are enjoying unspeakable happiness in Heaven! And as for me, I am lost forever, and that through my own fault, for I had at my disposal a superabundance of means of salvation.

But now repentance is unavailing, it is too late!"

But let us consider the expressions of regret of the various lost sinners. Their sorrow is vain, for, like that of Judas, it is the sorrow of despair.

"During life," these lost sinners will say to themselves, "I loved ease and comfort and luxury, fine garments, costly jewellery and princely mansions. To gain these I did not scruple to defraud my neighbour in every available way. I stole from my employers, I took false oaths, I joined secret societies, I even sold my virtue! I stayed away from Mass, I ate meat on forbidden days, I neglected the Sacraments, I went so far as to deny my faith. I contracted marriage before a civil magistrate, or before a heretical minister; I contracted a mixed marriage without dispensation; I got a divorce and then ventured to break the laws of

God and of the Church by getting married again! I wished to be free, to do just as I pleased.

The laws of God and of His Church forbade me to frequent dangerous occasions, and I spurned these laws because I wished to enjoy myself and gratify my passions by going with persons and into places that were dangerous to me, and thus I fell repeatedly into sins, even the most shameful.

God commanded me to be pure and chaste, and I took delight in gratifying my basest passions in every possible way, and sought every occasion of doing so. How criminally I acted in neglecting to give my children a religious education, and thus caused them to lose their souls! During life I was fond of listening to and joining in backbiting, calumny, obscene discourses, and even irreligious conversations. I loved to read filthy novels and to gaze on immodest pictures and objects. While on earth, I yielded to my passion for strong drink, and indulged in it to excess, until I degraded myself below the brute and committed crimes innumerable against my wife and children, against my neighbour.

During life I delighted in cursing, swearing, in uttering fearful oaths and imprecations and in quarrelling, in gambling and in almost every crime.

And now I find myself in the gloomy prison of Hell, in company of a countless multitude of villains, murderers, of the most degraded beings that have ever livedI have no longer a loving parent, a loving child, a sympathizing friend. No; all the ties of friendship, all the ties of nature, are forever broken, forever turned into devilish hate. Every evil spirit, every reprobate insults me, curses me, tortures me, seeks to make me suffer the more. I must submit to all this, because during life I refused to submit to the holy will of God. I could so easily have been saved, and now I am lost, lost forever, and that through my own fault! Never shall I see God, never shall I enjoy the delights of Heaven, never more shall I be released from these terrible torments. It is now too late!"

All this, and much more, will the worm of conscience say to the damned, stinging him with reproaches so relentlessly that he will almost be driven crazy with despair. In fact, the damned will rave and rage as if they were possessed, and will invoke curses on themselves. But all in vain; it is too late for repentance. This terrible remorse will do nothing towards atoning for their sins, it will only add to their anguish.

Consider this, obdurate sinner, who dost sin so boldly, and even when thy conscience pricks thee, turnest a deaf ear to its reproaches. Be assured that one day thy own conscience will be thy tormentor, and will plague thee more pertinaciously than the demons themselves. If thou dost desire to escape this never–ending misery, listen to the voice of conscience now, follow its counsel when it bids thee abstain from doing evil, and urges thee to do that which is right.

VIII. On Eternity

IN the preceding pages some slight portrayal of the torments of Hell has been placed before the reader; now eternity is the subject that must occupy our attention, one on which it is not easy to write or speak. The torments of Hell are all so horrible, so appalling, that they are enough to make the bravest man tremble. But the thought of eternity is so awful that the serious consideration of it is almost enough to deprive one of one s senses. For in this world, however afflicted a man may be, he has one sure source of solace, the knowledge that, sooner or later, his misery will end.

It appertains to human nature to get weary of everything after a time, even things that are agreeable to our nature and suited to our taste. If a man were forced to sit all day long at table, he would get a disgust of the viands before him. If one were made to sleep day and night for a whole week in the softest and most comfortable bed, how long the time would seem to him. If the most ardent lover of the dance were compelled to continue this favourite amusement day and night without rest, he would acquire a strong distaste for it.

And if this is the case with things that are congenial to our nature and inclinations, what would it be in regard to those which are unpleasant and repugnant to us? If a small stone got into one s shoe, and if as a penance one had to keep it there for a whole week, this would seem almost intolerable. And if a slight pain or inconvenience becomes terribly irksome after a time, how can a serious illness, or real discomfort, be borne continually without murmuring and impatience?

If it were possible that a wretched sinner could be condemned to lie in a furnace, bound hand and foot, for a whole year, would not the suffering deprive him of reason? No one could be so hard hearted as not to feel the deepest compassion for any one thus tormented.

Now look down into the abyss of Hell, and there thou wilt see thousands and thousands of these unhappy creatures in the lake of fire and torment. Many of them have already spent twenty, a hundred, a thousand, even five thousand years in this dreadful state of suffering.

But what is before them? Not five thousand years more, not a hundred thousand, not a thousand thousand of this terrible agony, they must endure it forever and ever; an eternity is before them, with out comfort or solace, without grace or mercy, without merit or recompense, without the faintest hope of deliverance. This is what renders the torment of the damned so immeasurable; this is what drives them to fury and despair.

What dost thou imagine that eternity really is, or what its duration will be? Eternity is something that has no beginning and no end. It is time which is always present and never passes away. Thus the torments of the damned will never end, never pass away. When a thousand years have gone by, another thousand will commence, and so on for evermore. None of the damned can reckon how long they have been in Hell, because there is no succession of day and night, no division of time, but continual and eternal night from the first moment of their entrance into Hell for ever more. And if thou wouldst conceive some faint idea of eternity, suppose the whole terrestrial globe to be composed of millet seeds, and suppose that every year a bird came, and picked out one of those tiny seeds, what an infinite number of years must elapse before the whole earth was eaten up in this way. Nay, how many thousand years must pass before one little hillock was consumed. It is impossible to make any estimate of the number.

Thou mayst perhaps think that it would take all eternity to destroy the earth by that slow process. But believe me, it might be destroyed many times over before eternity could end. For the earth must at last come to an end, even if only once in a century one single grain was taken from the whole, but eternity cannot end, for nothing can be taken from it.

How terrible is this thought ! It is indeed appalling when one attempts to realize it.

The damned would be joyful, they would give God thanks, if they could hope, after millions and millions of years of torment, to be at last released from their misery.

But there is no hope at all of their final release from the pains of Hell. No one who thinks seriously of this can fail to be awestruck and horrified. O God, how terrible Thou art ! How great is Thy severity! How canst Thou, the Father of mercies, see these unhappy creatures condemned to such punishments forever and ever, how canst Thou hear unmoved their despairing cries!

All this teaches us how grievous every mortal sin must be, since Thou, the all–merciful God, canst sentence the sinner to eternal damnation for one mortal sin. O Christian, I beseech thee, in the name of all that is holy, do not sin so lightly, do not think so little of mortal sin, see how dreadful is the chastisement inflicted upon the unfortunate sinners. It may perhaps appear scarcely credible to thee that God, whose mercies are infinite, could possibly inflict upon one of His frail creatures a never–ending punishment for one single mortal sin.

Yet so it is; and it is even true that a man who has led a pious life will, if before his death he should have the unspeakable misfortune to commit a mortal sin, and die impenitent, be consigned to eternal perdition.

The Psalmist could not help expressing his astonishment at this ; in fact he appears to think it hardly possible. Listen to his words: "I thought upon the days of old, and I had in my mind the eternal years. And I meditated in the night with my own heart, and I was exercised and I swept my spirit. Will God then cast off forever? or will He never be more favourable again? or will He cut off His mercy forever, from generation to generation ? or will God forget to show mercy? or will He in His anger shut up His mercies?" (Ps. Ixxvi. 6–10.) In another Psalm he answers these questions : " Man shall not give to God his ransom, nor the price of the redemption of his soul; he shall labour forever, and still live unto the end," that is to say he shall be tormented forever, and yet live on (Ps. xlviii. 9, 10).

The reason wherefore the all–merciful God punishes mortal sin with an eternal punishment, and nevermore pardons it, is because the sinner, when he is damned, will not awaken contrition and sorrow within his heart, or ask forgiveness of God. For if any one dies in mortal sin, he is so hardened in it, that he will not desist from it to all eternity. And because God has consigned him to perdition, he conceives so intense a hatred against Him, that he would injure Him in every way that he could.

Rather than humble himself before God, and implore His pardon, he would endure yet greater tortures in Hell. Therefore because the sinner will not repent of his sins, nor ask pardon for his sins, he remains eternally in a state of sin, and because his sin is never expiated or repented of, the punishment is likewise eternal.

For God does not cease to punish until the sinner repents and bewails his sin and asks for forgiveness.

Hence it will be seen that God does no wrong to the reprobate when He subjects him to everlasting chastisement, for Divine justice demands that if the sin is eternal in its duration, the penalty of that sin must likewise be eternal.

It may perhaps be surmised that the damned grow accustomed to their torments, and at length become insensitive and almost indifferent to them.

This is far from being the case. The damned feel their torture to its full extent, and always in the same degree. Each one of the miserable denizens of Hell feels his sufferings now as acutely as he did in the first hour of his damnation, and he will continue to feel them no less keenly after thou sands and thousands of years have elapsed.

Now because the damned know perfectly well that they will never be released from Hell, but must remain there forever; because they know that the dreadful tortures they endure will never end; because they know that no created being will ever compassionate them, but all will acknowledge the justice of their doom ; for this cause they begin to despair, and to curse themselves and all that the hand of God has created.

Their despair only augments their sufferings. This we see from the example of our fellow creatures on earth, if they give way to despair. It is impossible to do anything with a man who is in despair; no one can help or console him, no one can comfort him or bring him to reason. He looks like a spectre ; he raves and rages like the very devil himself; he declares he will put an end to his life, that he will drown himself or hang himself; he destroys everything that comes in his way; he curses all men and all things. This the damned do in their despair, and thereby they torture themselves even more than the devils can torture them. They shriek and howl, they curse and swear, they storm and rage; in fact, they behave just as if they were fiends incarnate.

In their fury and spite they attack one another with the fiercest animosity; nay, they endeavour by every possible means to strangle themselves in their frantic despair.

Their efforts are, however, futile. All that they accomplish is to increase their torment, and inflict on themselves fresh pains.

Would that every obdurate sinner would lay this to heart, and take heed, lest one day he become the prey of this eternal despair.

"It is a fearful thing to fall into the hands of the living God," says St. Paul (Heb. x. 31). If we now dread Hell, we shall not have any reason to fear or endure it in the next life.

Every one has sufficient grounds for dreading it. The just and holy should fear Hell, because they may yet fall into it. So long as they remain on earth, they are surrounded by not only exterior, but also interior, dangers. Outside of them there is the world with its allurements, its scandals and temptations, and human respect.

Within them dwell violent passions and a weak will. Only a single mortal sin suffices to cause their condemnation to the infernal abyss. How many are now in Hell, who for a time were remarkable for their piety and virtue, but who gradually grew careless in the service of God, and finally fell into mortal sin and died without having become reconciled with God. Even the great St. Teresa was in danger of damnation, for God showed her the place destined for her in Hell, if she did not give up certain faults.

The greatest Saints have shuddered and trembled at the thought of the danger they were in of committing mortal sin and of being condemned for it to the endless torments of Hell. St. Peter of Alcantara, who performed such great penances, dreaded even in his last moments the danger of falling into Hell. St. Augustine and St. Bernard were filled with terror at the very thought of Hell and of the danger they were in of deserving it.

The careless, the lukewarm Catholic should, above all, dread Hell, for he is continually walking on the brink of the infernal abyss. He makes little of the precepts of hearing Mass, of the prescribed abstinence from flesh meat, he scruples not neglecting the religious training of his children, he associates with persons and frequents places that are to him an occasion of sin, he yields to impure thoughts, commits sins of impurity without remorse, gives way to his vindictive feelings against his neighbour, appropriates to himself the goods of his neighbour, indulges to excess in eating and drinking, neglects prayer and the Sacraments. Now is the time for him to be aroused from his life of sin, now is the time for him to give up sin and change his life, for if he defers doing so, it may soon be too late. This may, indeed, be the last warning that God gives him. Oh, if the damned could come back to life, to what penances and austerities would they not eagerly and cheerfully submit!

The prophet Isaias asks: "Which of you can dwell with devouring fire?" (Is. xxxiii. 14.) Canst thou stand the fearful torments of Hell for all eternity, thou who art so fond of comfort and so sensitive to the least pain? Which of you has deserved to dwell in Hell? Every one of us already deserved, immediately after our first mortal sin, to be condemned to that abyss of misery and woe ! It is owing to the Divine mercy that we have not been so condemned.

"Unless the Lord had been my helper, my soul had almost dwelt in Hell" (Ps. xciii. 17). We are certain of having deserved Hell, but we are not so certain of having been forgiven. "Man knoweth not whether he be worthy of love or hatred" (Eccles. ix. i). What a dreadful uncertainty? How much should it cause us to tremble!

Isaias asks again (xxxiii. 14): "Which of you shall dwell with everlasting burnings?" The answer is : All those sinners who do not give up sin, who do not bewail and confess their sins and amend their life, shall dwell with everlasting burnings!

Let us, dear reader, make every effort, strain every nerve, undergo every suffering, make every sacrifice in this life, that we may escape the horrible fate of those who fall victims, through their own fault, to the Divine justice! No pain is too great, no sacrifice is too dear, when there is question of avoiding eternal torments. Let us then say with St. Augustine: "Lord, burn us here, cut and bruise us in this life, provided Thou spare us in eternity!"

PART IV

ON HEAVEN

I. On the Nature of Heaven

WE must not, as some do, picture to ourselves Heaven as a purely spiritual realm. For Heaven is a definite place, where not only God is, and the Angels now are, but where Christ is also in His sacred humanity, and Our Lady with her human body. There, too, all the blessed will dwell with their glorified bodies after the Last Judgment. If Heaven is a definite locality, it must accordingly be a visible, not a spiritual kingdom ; for a place must in its nature be to some extent conformable to those who abide in it.

Besides, we know that after the Last Judgment he Saints will behold Heaven with their bodily eyes, and consequently it must be a visible kingdom. We are ignorant of what the material structure of Heaven will be composed, we only know that it will be something infinitely superior to and more costly than the matter of which the other spheres, the sun, the moon, and other heavenly bodies, are formed.

For since God has created Heaven for Himself and for His elect, He has made it so beautiful and so glorious that the blessed will never tire of the contemplation of its splendours to all eternity.

Yet, I repeat, it is not within the power of the writer to describe, nor within that of the reader to comprehend, what it is of which Heaven is actually composed. Something may perhaps be learned concerning this from what St. Teresa writes. Speaking of herself, she says : " The Blessed Mother of God gave me a jewel, and hung around my neck a superb golden chain, to which a cross of priceless value was attached. Both the gold and the precious stones thus given to me are so unlike those which we have here in this world that no comparison can be instituted between them. They are beautiful beyond anything that can be conceived, and the matter whereof they are composed is beyond our knowledge. For what we call gold and precious stones beside them appear dark and lustreless as charcoal."

From these words we may form some idea of the beauty, the rarity, the costly nature of the stones wherewith the walls of Heaven are built. We gather from them that the light of Heaven is so dazzling as not only to eclipse the sun and stars, but to cause all earthly brightness to appear as darkness. We have besides every reason to believe that in the light of Heaven all the colors of the rainbow are seen to flash, giving it an indescribable charm to the eyes of the blessed. Moreover, the bodies of the redeemed are resplendent with light, and the more Saintly their life on earth has been, the more brilliantly do they shine in Heaven.

What must be the glory of that celestial firmament, glittering with the radiance of many thousand stars! Nothing is more pleasing to the eye than light ; how brilliant, how beautiful must the light of Heaven be since, compared with it, the sun s bright rays are but darkness.

How the redeemed must delight in the contemplation of this clear and dazzling brightness.

O my God, grant me grace that on earth I may love the light and eschew the works of darkness, in order that I may attain to the contemplation of the eternal and perpetual light !

Concerning the size of Heaven all we know isthat it is immeasurable, inconceivable, incomprehensible.

A learned Divine, speaking on this subject, says : " If God were to make every grain of sand into a new world, all these innumerable spheres would not fill the immensity of Heaven." St. Bernard also says that we are warranted in the belief that every one of the saved will have a place and an inheritance of no narrow limits assigned him in the celestial country.

How immeasurably vast in extent must Heaven then be ! Well may the prophet Baruch exclaim : " O Israel, how great is the house of God, and how vast is the place of His possession 1 It is great and hath no end ; it is high and immense " (Baruch iii. 24, 25).

We can readily believe this, for we have before our eyes the boundless realms of space. But of the nature of the infinite realms of Heaven we know nothing, and yet we can to some extent picture them to our imagination. It would be against common sense to think that these vast celestial domains are empty and bare, that the great Artificer, to whom the creation of worlds is a very little thing, would leave them unbeautified and unadorned.

If princes and lords fill every space, and leave no corner in their palaces or their grounds unembellished and unadorned, shall we suppose that the great King of Heaven would permit His regal palace, His celestial paradise, to be lacking in magnificence and in beauty ? What would there be to delight the senses of the Saints if Heaven were a large empty space ? What enjoyment, except the beatificvision of God, would there be for them, if they stood all together in a barren plain, like sheep in a penfold ? Are we not justified in believing that there are splendid and spacious mansions in Heaven constructed of incorruptible materials ?

Nay, more, a learned expositor of Holy Scripture considers it probable that by the wondrous skill and wisdom of the great Creator, these fair palaces and dwellings are of varied form and size, some being lower, others higher, some more richly adorned than others. Towering above all, and surpassing all in grandeur and magnificence, the palace of the great King Jesus Christ stands pre–eminent; and next in splendour and dignity ranks the abode of our Sovereign Lady, the Queen of Heaven. Then come the twelve palaces of the twelve apostles, which are so rich and beautiful that Heaven itself marvels at their magnificence. Besides these are mansions and dwellings innumerable which render the heavenly Jerusalem indescribably imposing and attractive. These splendid abodes were created when Heaven itself was made, and destined to be the dwellings of the redeemed.

The Church teaches us, in the office for martyrs, that each one of the elect will have his own place in the kingdom of Heaven. Dabo sanctis meis locum nominatum in regno Patris mei, dicit Dominus. (In 2 noct. Antiph. I. de Com. pi. Martj.) " I will give to My Saints an appointed place in the kingdom of My Father." And the Royal Psalmist says: " The Saints shall rejoice in glory; they shall be joyful in their beds " (Ps. cxlix. 5).

We have also Christ s words : " Make unto you friends of the mammon of iniquity; that when you shall fail, they may receive you into everlasting dwellings ; " that is to say, spend what you have over and above on works of charity and benevolence, that these may prove as friends to you, who will obtain for you admittance into the eternal and celestial dwellings (Luke xvi. 9).

Again : " In My Father's house there are many mansions." Hence it may be inferred that each one of the redeemed has his separate abode in Heaven. For as a just and prudent father divides his real and personal property amongst his children, assigning to each one his particular share, so our heavenly Father apportions to each of His elect a part of His celestial treasures, both visible and invisible, giving to each one more or less, according to the amount he deserves to receive.

Who shall describe the majesty and glory of these heavenly mansions? If the kings and princes of this world build grand and costly palaces for themselves, what must be the splendour and beauty of the celestial city which the King of kings has built for Himself and those who love Him and are His friends ? Hear what St. John says concerning this city: "An Angel showed me the holy city Jerusalem, having the glory of God. The light thereof was like to a precious stone, as to the jasper stone, even as crystal. The city itself was of pure gold, like unto glass, and the foundations of the wall of the city were adorned with all manner of precious stones " (Apoc. xxi. u, 18, 19).

Speaking of the size of the city, the same apostle writes : " The Angel that spoke with me had a measure of a reed of gold, to measure the city and the gates thereof, and the wall. And the city lieth in a four–square, and the length thereof is as great as the breadth ; and he measured the city with the golden reed for twelve thousand furlongs, and the height and the breadth thereof are equal. And he measured the wall thereof an hundred forty–four cubits, the measure of a man, and used by the Angel."

A furlong is two hundred and twenty yards, and eight furlongs make a mile. It must be observed that the Angel did not measure the circumference of the city, but only the length of the wall, which was twelve thousand furlongs. When this is multiplied by four, it gives forty–eight thousand furlongs as the circumference of the city, that is equivalent to six thousand miles. To people a city of this size many thousand millions of inhabitants would be needed.

From the information given by St. John, who tells us that the length, the breadth, and the height of the city are equal, we form some idea of the imposing height of this celestial structure. This city does not constitute the whole of the heavenly Jerusalem, it is the special dwelling place of the most high God, wherein the sacred humanity of Christ abides, together with many companies of Angels and of the most eminent Saints. For besides this august city, there are others innumerable in the heavenly plains, wherein the redeemed dwell in the society of Angels. The more good a Saint has done on earth, the grander is the residence assigned him in Heaven. These palaces and mansions are transparent as crystal and built of precious stones of the costliest kind. And we may add on the authority of a learned theologian, that the blessed hold intercourse with one another, and meet together to laud and magnify the omnipotence of the Most High, who prepared for them such glorious abodes, and join in extolling His wisdom and His love.

Dost thou not, O my soul, feel an intense longing to behold this heavenly city, and, what is more, to dwell therein for evermore ? We esteem it a pleasure to visit a fine city, renowned for its architectural and other attractions ; and many are the travellers who journey all over the world to see foreign towns, and feast their eyes on their beauty. What are these cities of earth in comparison with the celestial cities? Could we but look into it for a few moments only, what wondrous things we should behold ! We should assuredly exclaim, in the words of King David: "How lovely are Thy tabernacles, O Lord of hosts! My soul longeth and fainteth for the courts of the Lord. My heart and my flesh have rejoiced in the living God. Blessed are they that dwell in Thy house, O Lord; they shall praise thee forever and ever. For better is one day in Thy courts above thousands; I have chosen to be an abject in the house of my God rather than to dwell in the tabernacles of sinners" (Ps. Ixxxiii.).

If we may venture to speak of the interior of the celestial realm, we may assume that the vast, immeasurable space of Heaven does not only contain these heavenly cities, but much more besides, all of which enhances the delights of that blissful land. For as kings and princes on earth have gardens and pleasure grounds laid out beside their palaces, where they amuse themselves in the summer season, so, many theologians assert, there are heavenly paradises, that afford increased delight to the blessed.

For not only the souls of the saved, but their glorified bodies also, will be conducted by the Angels of God into Heaven after the Day of Judgment.

St. Augustine, St. Anselm, and many other Saints do not hesitate to maintain that there are in Heaven real trees, real fruits, and real flowers, indescribably attractive and delightful to the sight, taste, smell, and touch, different from anything we can imagine.

In the revelations of the Saints mention is made of the gardens in Heaven, and the flowers that blossom there ; and we know it is recorded in the legend of St. Dorothea, that she sent to Theophilus by the hands of an Angel a basket of flowers culled in the gardens of the celestial paradise, of such surpassing beauty that the sight of them led him to become a Christian, and lay down his life for the faith of Christ.

We also read in the life of St. Didacus, that on coming to himself after a trance into which he fell shortly before his death, he cried aloud : " O what flowers there are in Paradise ! what flowers there are in paradise ! " Similar incidents are frequently to be met with in the legends of the Saints.

Consider how delightful it will be for the happy ones who are saved to wander in the celestial gardens, and contemplate those fair flowers. How pleasing the lovely blossoms are to the eye, how delicious is the fragrance they exhale ! Of a truth, if a man were to obtain possession of a single one of these heavenly flowers, it would produce on him the same effect as on Theophilus. He would be spoiled for all the beauty of earth, and would strive with his whole soul after the perfect beauty of Heaven.

Meditate often, therefore, upon the things of Heaven; raise thy eyes and thy heart to the bright firmament above, and awaken within thy heart by this or other means a keen desire to behold the mansions of the eternal Father, and to dwell in them for evermore.

O God, who hast enriched the heavenly Jerusalem with such beauty in order that we poor children of earth might have a greater longing to behold it, I beseech Thee, inflame my heart with an ardent affection and longing for the celestial abode which Thou hast prepared for us. For blessed are they, O Lord, who dwell in Thy house ; they shall enjoy consummate felicity for evermore, and for evermore they will praise the power, the wisdom, the bounty of our God. Would that I were worthy to be associated with that sinless company, to behold that fair city, to become one of its happy denizens. Grant me this grace, O God, I pray Thee; let me not be excluded from the number of Thine elect.

O blessed Saints of God, you who dwell within the courts of the heavenly Jerusalem, I humbly entreat you to intercede for me, that in His infinite clemency the God of mercy may grant me so to live that I may be found worthy to be admitted to your blissful company.

Hear the prayers of Thy Saints, O most compassionate God, and through the merits of Jesus Christ give me a share in that inheritance which He purchased for us with His precious blood. May the things of this world lose all value in my eyes, and do Thou make my heart to glow with the burning desire to behold Thee and the city that Thou hast built, the heavenly Jerusalem. Amen.

II. On the Joys of Heaven

Now that we have meditated upon the heavenly Jerusalem, the city of God, we will proceed to consider the happiness which the Saints who dwell therein enjoy, both in regard to body and soul. It is true as yet they have not their bodies, as a general rule, but at the Last Day they will all have them again, and those bodies will then be so beauteous, that nothing in the world can compare with them. And this will principally be because every member will be endowed with four qualities or attributes, namely: beauty, impassibility, agility, and subtlety. By reason of its beauty or glory the body of each one of the elect will shine like a star, yet, as one star differs from another in glory, so the Saints will shine with greater or less splendour, according as their lives upon earth have been more or less holy.

In these glorified and radiant bodies the blessed will be so inexpressibly beautiful, that if a mortal man were now to behold one of these resplendent beings, he would be dazzled by its brilliance and be ready to expire for joy of heart.

In her revelations to St. Bridget, the Blessed Mother of God once said: "The Saints stand around my Son like countless stars, whose glory is not to be compared with any temporal light. Believe me, if the Saints could be seen shining with the glory they now possess, no human eye could endure their light all would turn away, dazzled and blinded."

Think what happiness it will be for thee, when thy body shines like the sun at midday. Everything that lives and moves rejoices in the light and warmth of the sun: it gladdens all the face of nature. In like manner thy body will be a joy and delight to thyself and all around thee in Heaven, because of its beauty and its glory.

The second attribute is impassibility, for the glorified body is incapable of suffering. It will never be sick or infirm, it will not grow old or unsightly. It will never again be inconvenienced by hunger or thirst, by heat or cold, by draught or dampness. It can nevermore be burned by fire, drowned in water, wounded by the sword or crushed beneath a weight; it will be immortal, unchangeable, eternally endowed with perfect health and unfailing strength. If any one on earth could purchase this gift of impassibility, how gladly would he give all he possessed to obtain it!

The third attribute is agility. The glorified body will be able to traverse the greatest distance with the speed of thought. In one moment it can come down from Heaven to earth; in one moment it can pass from one end of the Heavens to the other, without labour, without fatigue, without difficulty. We often wish that we could fly like the birds, that we could speed on our way like clouds on the wings of the wind, that we could follow thought in its rapid flight. If it were possible to purchase this power, every one would part with all his worldly wealth for it, if only to obtain it for one single year.

How is it, then, that thou dost take so little trouble to ensure for thyself the possession of this gift for all eternity?

The fourth attribute of the glorified body is subtlety, which consists in the faculty of penetrating all matter, of passing in and out wheresoever it will. No wall is so thick, no iron gate so massive, no mountain so great as to form an obstacle to the glorified body. As the sun s rays pass through glass, so the bodies of the redeemed as they are in Heaven, penetrate all matter, however dense and solid it may be. They can also make themselves visible or invisible at will. What wouldst thou not give to become possessed of such a faculty?

How great is Thy bounty, almighty God, towards Thine elect ! Thou be stowest upon them precious and sublime gifts, that no amount of this world's riches can purchase. Who would not gladly spend his life in Thy service and suffer afflictions in this world in order to possess these inestimable gifts to all eternity?

Ask this poor frail body if it would not fain shine as the light, be exempt from suffering, move with the speed of thought, be unfettered as a spirit? To own such powers would indeed be a joy and a consolation unspeakable.

Wouldst thou not consent to have a hard penance laid on thee for a whole year, if at the end these attributes were bestowed on thee? If so, then do not esteem it a grievance to lead here below a life of penance, in the hope that these fair gifts may be thine during all eternity. See that here on earth thou love the light, the light of good works; bear all pain and tribulation with patience, be prompt and zealous in the service of God; mortify within thyself more and more all sensual desires, and thou wilt assuredly be the happy possessor hereafter of these four attributes of the glorified body.

We will now turn our attention to the pleasure and gratification which the blessed will experience by means of these five senses ; and first of all we will inquire what satisfaction they will find in their sight. The power of sight will be so perfect that nothing can be hid from their eyes. They will see what is distant as distinctly as what is near, the smallest object as plainly as the largest, the dark will be to them as clear as the light Their vision will be so undimmed that they will be able to gaze without flinching at the sun, even were its light a hundredfold more dazzling. Their sight will be so keen that no obstacle will offer a hindrance to it.Now think what delight awaits thy sense of sight, when thy eyes first rest upon the glories of Heaven.First they will behold the city itself, with its palaces and mansions, whereof the splendour and majesty is so great that the contemplation of these magnificent structures would afford pleasurable employment for a whole eternity.

In the second place, thou wilt gaze with delight upon the fair flowers, the trees, the gardens, and all the other beauteous sights that will arrest the eye in Heaven.

Thirdly, it will be an unspeakable pleasure to thee to behold thyself and all the other Saints arrayed in beauty, glory, splendour, grace and majesty far surpassing anything seen in this world.

Fourthly, thou wilt see the incomparable beauty of the Angels, for it is believed that those celestial spirits will assume bodies of great loveliness formed from the air, in order to render themselves visible to the blessed. This opinion is held by St. Anselm. And if the beauty of an Angel immeasurably exceeds all human beauty, wilt thou not rejoice in the contemplation of so many thousands of Angelic beings, all of surpassing loveliness, for all eternity?

Fifthly, on nothing will thine eyes rest with such keen delight as on the inexpressible beauty of Jesus and Mary, whose glorified bodies are so irresistibly charming, attractive, beautiful and majestic, that if the damned were permitted to behold them, they would no longer find Hell intolerable.

Now consider what a fertile source of delight it will be, to be continually and forever surrounded by sights so enchanting and so sublime. Our natural inclination leads us here below to take long journeys for the sake of seeing some beauteous sight, to expend large sums to obtain some beauteous object, and even to imperil our souls in our eager search after what is beautiful.

Since the love of the beautiful is so deeply rooted in our nature, how strange that we do not yearn for the beauty of Heaven. Why do we not close our eyes to the attractions of earth, that we may be found worthy to open them upon the splendours of Heaven?

From sight let us pass on to hearing.

It would be unwise were we to attempt to describe the gratification it will be to the ear to hear the canticles of the Angels, and the soft music of their harps. The nine choirs of Angels will sing the praise of God, and the blessed will join them not only in heart, for they will mingle their voices also in the sweet harmony. Thus the powers of both soul and body will be exercised, and the praises of God will ascend in melodious hymns and celestial songs.

For if we mortals are impelled by fervent love and heartfelt joy to lift our voice in song, how much more will the holy Angels and blessed Saints do so, who are all aflame with the love of God, and filled with joy unspeakable. Their hymns of praise will resound without ceasing through the courts of Heaven.

In a prophetic spirit the elder Tobias says: "The gates of Jerusalem shall be built of sapphire and of emerald, and all the walls thereof round about with precious stones, all its streets shall be paved with white and clean stones, and alleluia shall be sung in its streets" (Tob. xiii. 21, 22).

These words seem to indicate that the redeemed will walk at their pleasure with one another in the heavenly Jerusalem, their voices uniting in happy alleluias.

In wondrous harmony the Angels and Saints will praise and magnify their God. What happiness for them, O my God, what sweetness, what joy! If sweet songs rejoice us here, and awaken elevated feelings within our breast, the canticles of the Angels and Saints will indeed cause us rapture and delight, when we have the felicity to be admitted into their blessed company.

My God and my all ! how great is the abundance of the favours Thou hast prepared for them that love Thee! My heart thirsts for the stream of celestial joys. Truly blessed are they that dwell in Thy house, O Lord; they shall praise Thee forever and ever. The Saints shall rejoice and be glad in this glory, the high praises of God shall be in their mouth. Would that it were even now granted me to join these citizens of Heaven and with them to extol Thy name forever! When will the hour come, that happy hour in which I shall be privileged to behold the majesty of Thy house? Until it comes, I shall bear all the sufferings and tribulations of this world with patience, and will brighten my journey through this valley of tears by singing Thy praise; I will bless the Lord at all times, His praise shall be ever in my mouth. Magnify the Lord with me, ye Angels and Saints; let us extol His name evermore.

From the sense of hearing we will pass on to that of smell. The delicious odours of paradise surpass anything that man can imagine. The fairest lilies, roses, violets, carnations, and other rare and lovely flowers grow in the gardens of the heavenly paradise, and their fragrance is so delightful, that if a man had but a petal of one of those flowers, he would be overcome by the sweetness of the perfume. "Israel [that is the company of the redeemed] shall spring as the lily, and his smell shall be that of Libanus" (Osee xiv. 6).

Experience has abundantly shown that the bodies of the Saints whilst in their graves already emit a fragrant smell; how much more powerful will that fragrance be when they are again raised to life andglorified. Above all the bodies of Christ and of His Blessed Mother will exhale so sweet a perfume that all Heaven will be pervaded by it.

How lovely are Thy tabernacles, O Lord, wherein we shall be invigorated by the aromatic odours that environ us ! For if sweet odours refresh and revive us here below, the odours of Paradise will surely give strength and refreshment to the blessed.

Even the sense of taste will be gratified in Heaven, not, it is true, by the consumption of ordinary food, but in a manner whereof we can as yet form no conjecture. The blessed will taste a sweet sustenance which will satisfy them, as we learn from the words of the Royal Psalmist: "They shall be inebriated with the plenty of Thy house, Thou shalt make them drink of the torrent of Thy pleasure" (Ps. xxxv. 9).

The sense of touch will have its own peculiar enjoyment. The more one has mortified himself here on earth, the greater will be his bodily well–being hereafter. St. Anselm says: "In the future life the Saints will experience a feeling of untold comfort and ease. This pleasurable sensation will pervade every member, producing a wondrous sense of peace and contentment."

In fact, what can be wanting to the glorified body in Heaven? It is in the enjoyment of perpetual health, perpetual rest, perpetual happiness, so that in the superabundance of joy and satisfactionit can scarce realize how enviable is its condition.

Finally, the redeemed will take very great pleasure in beholding one another, in conversing with one another, in kindly intercourse and friendly communication. Think how beautiful a sight it will be to see hundreds of thousands of beings in all the splendour of their glorified state. If on earth we esteem it a pleasure to look upon a handsome face, we can appreciate in some slight degree what it will be in Heaven, the lowliest of whose inhabitants is possessed of a beauty far exceeding the personal attractions of any mortal man.

Moreover, the redeemed are united together by the bond of mutual charity, for they love one another more dearly than the most affectionate of brothers and sisters. If they have never met on earth, yet they know one another better than if they had been brought up together. Each one will know the incidents of his earthly career.

Each one will be able to see into the other s heart, and know how great is the affection he feels for him. Each one will rejoice in the other s glory as much as if it were his own; and the lowliest in the kingdom of Heaven exults as much in the glory of the highest as the latter can possibly do. This was explained to St. Augustine by St. John the Baptist in a vision. "Know," he said to him, "that on account of the inexpressible charity that the blessed have towards one another, that each takes no less pleasure in the exaltation of another than if it were his own. Nay, more, he who is greater wishes that the lower were equal to him, and even more honoured than himself ; for in his triumph he, too, would triumph.

"In like manner those who are in a lowly place rejoice in the glory of those who are in the highest place; they do not envy them, far from it. They would not desire the high position if the others had it not; they would rather give them a part of their own glory, were this possible." Hence it may be seen that the Saints take pleasure in the splendour wherewith their fellows are crowned, and entertain for each and all of them a heartfelt affection. More especially do they love one who has, by word or example, helped them on their way to Heaven; to such a one they know not how they can sufficiently testify their gratitude.

Each one will also feel a particular affection for the Saint whom he chose as his patron upon earth, and whom he honoured with a special devotion; and this affection will be reciprocated by the object of it. Those who stood in this relation to one another will meet together more often; they will converse on holy subjects and mutually relate their experiences on earth, telling how marvellously the providence of God saved them from eternal perdition. In a word, the pleasures afforded to the redeemed by this intercourse will be innumerable, and they will do everything in their power to gratify and show kindness to one another.

O God of all mercies! who would not desire to enter into this land of eternal peace, where are joys beyond all that mortal man can conceive, joys so many and so manifold, so wondrous and so sweet! Sometimes the pleasures of this world have such a fascination for a man, that he cannot renounce them, even though he sees Hell open before him. And yet those pleasures are less than nothing in comparison with the joys of Heaven; in fact, all the joys one can picture to one s self or desire for one s self cannot equal the least and the lowest of the joys that will be ours to all eternity! O my God, how unspeakable will be the bliss of Heaven ! May it be my happy lot to share in that felicity!

Urged by this desire, I will give Thee no rest, every day I will implore Thee to take me to Thyself. I will detach my heart from this world, I will entirely renounce all earthly pleasures; all my aspirations, all my affections shall be fixed upon the heavenly treasures, and I will hold myself ready every day to quit this earthly scene. The sooner death comes to fetch me hence, the more welcome will it be, for I shall leave this land of exile and enter into my true country. God grant that so it may be. Amen.

III. On the Joys of Heaven (Continued)

WITH regard to the spiritual joys of the redeemed in Heaven, they are in such great abundance, that in speaking of them one does not know where to begin or where to end. Think of the spiritual consolations granted to eminent servants of God in this world. We know concerning some Saints that their life on earth was more that of Angels than of men, so frequently were they favoured with ecstasies, visions, interior lights, and Divine consolations of all kinds. And yet all these favours were but as a drop out of the boundless ocean of celestial sweetness. What rapture it will be for holy souls in Heaven to drink from the fountain–head, and draw freely from the inexhaustible source of all felicity! All the powers of the mind, the understanding, the memory, the will, the imagination, every thought, every desire, the whole intellectual being, elevated and perfected by God Himself, will be fully satisfied, and will add to and heighten the joys of the soul.

With the understanding the blessed will behold all created things in the light of God, and thoroughly penetrate the secrets of nature. It is recorded of King Solomon that "God gave to Solomon wisdom and understanding exceeding much, as the sand that is on the seashore. And the wisdom of Solomon surpassed the wisdom of all the Orientals and of the Egyptians, and he was wiser than all men. He also spoke three thousand parables, and his poems were a thousand and five. And he treated about trees from the cedar that is in Lebanon unto the hyssop that cometh out of the wall ; and he discoursed of beasts, and of fowls, and of creeping things, and of fishes. And they came from all nations to hear the wisdom of Solomon, and from all the kings of the earth, who heard of his wisdom" (3 Kings iv. 29–34).

We have never heard of wisdom equal to this, nor can we cease to wonder at the wide range and astuteness of this great king s understanding. Yet compared with the wisdom of the least of the Saints in Heaven, it ranks no higher than does the knowledge possessed by a child of three years old beside the erudition and wisdom of the most learned of men. For all the operations of nature, all the powers of the universe are open and revealed to the least of the Saints in Heaven. Nothing is hidden or mysterious in his eyes. He knows all that the Holy Trinity has accomplished from all eternity, in how marvellous a manner the Heavens and the earth were created out of nothing, how wisely all has been ordered and maintained from the beginning to the end of time. He knows how the Son of God was begotten of the Father before all ages; he knows how the Holy Spirit proceeds eternally from the Father and the Son. He knows how Christ was born of an earthly mother without violation of her virginity; he knows all that Our Lord did and suffered during His whole life, and how each Saint and servant of God lived for God and laboured in His service. All that is mysterious and incomprehensible to us in the Holy Scriptures, the mysteries of religion and of nature, he understands without a moment s reflection. Hadst thou been on earth but a simple, illiterate peasant, on thy entrance into Heaven thy eyes would be opened, and thou wouldst see clearly and understand all things perfectly. What joy, what happiness this knowledge and clear insight will be to thee I What grateful thanks thou wilt render to God for it!

Secondly, in as far as their memory is concerned, the blessed will also find fullness of joy in Heaven, for it will, like the understanding, be enlightened by God; and all the events of their past life will be as fresh and as distinct to their remembrance as if they beheld them inscribed on tablets before their eyes. Then they perceive by what a marvellous way God led them to their eternal goal, how mercifully He pardoned their transgressions, how He succoured them in the hour of temptation, and how He made all things work together for their good.

This retrospect will arouse in the heart of each one the holiest gratitude towards God and oft–times they will give expression to it thus: O my God, whom I love above all things, how great are the gifts and graces Thou hast bestowed upon me, how generous Thou hast been towards me, how often Thou hast rescued me from the danger of falling into sin, how mercifully Thou hast preserved me from eternal damnation, and how wonderfully Thou hast guided me in the way of salvation ! How can I sufficiently praise and magnify Thine infinite bounty? How can I sufficiently thank Thee and adore Thee for the benefits Thou hast lavished on me?

Thirdly, the will of each one of the blessed will be crowned with felicity, and kindled with the love of God and of the blessed in whose company he is.

The noblest pleasures a man can enjoy come from his will. A man is happy when all succeeds with him according to his wishes; when he acquires and possesses all that his heart can desire; when he is generally esteemed and praised by his fellow–men; when he loves, and is loved by the object of his affections. This and much more besides is the portion of the blessed, but in the highest degree and in the greatest possible perfection.

The love of God for them, and their love of Him is so profound, that they are inflamed and consumed with Divine charity, that their will resembles a live coal, glowing with light and heat, until it is absorbed by the fire of which it is a part. So it is with the Saints in Heaven; imbued with Divine charity, they burn and shine in the light of God, and reflect His image more and more. St. John says: "We know that when He shall appear we shall be like to Him, be cause we shall see Him as He is" (i John iii. 2).

In the love of God and in union with Him they find such ineffable delight that, inebriated by the sweetness of Divine charity they lose themselves in Him.

There is no greater happiness upon earth than to love and be loved, and the more tender, pure and ardent this love is, the greater the joy and delight it affords us. Now the love of Heaven, the love of the redeemed for God and for one another, is the most tender, the most pure, the most ardent affection, an affection infinite and boundless; consequently it is a source of immense delight and happiness unspeakable. May the God of all grace make us partakers of this love, and we shall then know by experience that of which words fail to convey an idea. No one will be privileged to partake in this love, unless here below he lives in the love of God, and dies in His friendship. Let us therefore strive to increase within us this Divine charity, that we may be admitted hereafter to the full enjoyment of His love.

The beatific vision of the Divine countenance is a joy above all joys, a delight far surpassing all the celestial pleasures of which we have spoken. Without this all other joys would lose their savour, they would be changed to bitterness.

On one occasion, when the devil was speaking by the mouth of a person who was possessed, he said: "If the whole Heavens were a sheet of parchment, if the whole ocean were ink, if every blade of grass were pen, and every man on earth a scribe, it would not suffice to describe the intense, immeasurable delight which the vision of God affords to the blessed." And at another time he said that if God would but vouchsafe to grant him the privilege of beholding His Divine countenance for a few moments, he would, if it were possible, gladly bear in his own person all the torments of Hell until the Day of Judgment. This teaches us that if a man spent his whole life in works of most severe penance, and after his death were permitted only for one instant to gaze on the face of God, he would have received an ample recompense for all his mortifications.

Now consider how transcendent must be the bliss which the Saints derive from the contemplation, the enjoyment, the possession of the supreme God! If to gaze on the Divine countenance for one passing moment is a joy beyond all that a life of pleasure offers to the world ling, what rapture will it be to gaze for evermore, with undimmed eyes, on His infinite beauty, what rapture to call this supreme Good one's own for all eternity!

God is a being in whom all that is most admirable and desirable exists in the highest degree. In Him is all that most attracts and fascinates us; clemency, beauty, justice, compassion, wisdom, majesty, every sweet and sublime attribute in its fullest perfection. From God proceeds all grace, all that we need for our spiritual and temporal welfare, all the happiness, the joy, the repose, the consolation, all the benefits and blessings which His creatures enjoy in Heaven and on earth. And when the redeemed enter upon the contemplation of this infinite Good, upon the possession of this source of all that is to be loved and admired and longed for, their joy will indeed be full. What unspeakable delight it will afford them to understand the mystery of the Incarnation, the mystery of the Holy Eucharist!

What unspeakable delight it will be to them to comprehend how God can be invisible Himself, and yet see everything ; how He can Himself be unmoved, and yet the source of all motion; how He can be Himself immutable, and yet the author of all change. These and many other mysteries will be made clear to the blessed in the light of God, and this fount of knowledge will not be exhausted to all eternity. The more they know God, the more will their desire to know Him better increase, and of this knowledge there will be no limit and no defect.

Thus they will ever hunger, and yet be perfectly satisfied; this rich treasury will ever be open to them, and never will they exhaust all the wealth it contains.

Meditate frequently on this subject, O reader, and excite within thy soul an earnest desire to enjoy God forever and ever.

O my God and my all ! Who art infinite beauty, infinite sweetness, infinite bounty ! With all my heart I long after Thee. As the hart pants for the water–brooks, so my soul thirsts for Thee, the mighty and living God; when shall I come and appear before Thy presence? When will it be my happy lot to behold Thee, to enjoy Thee forever? I venture to hope that this joy may be mine; I humbly hope and trust in Thy infinite goodness, for Thou dost reject no one who comes to Thee with a contrite and loving heart. –How rich, how happy, how joyful shall I be when I shall have this supreme Good for my own possession 1 I shall embrace Thee with reverent affection, I shall lose myself in Thee, when once I have Thee for my own.

I am ready, I am desirous, O my God, to do all that lies in my power, to render myself worthy to be admitted into Thy presence. I am prepared to suffer all that my weak nature will enable me to bear. I am prepared to withdraw from the world, to renounce all earthly things in as far as the duties of my position permit. I am prepared to labour as far as in me lies, for Thy service ; and this I will do in the hope of winning Thee, the infinite and eternal Good, and beholding for evermore Thy infinite beauty. Nay, even did I know that I should be lost, I would still love Thee. For I do not love Thee because I hope for eternal salvation through Thee, but I love Thee because Thou art perfect Beauty and infinite Goodness, worthy to be the sole object of our affections and aspirations.

Thus believing and thus hoping, I desire to live and die, and I call the Angels and Saints to witness to the truth of what I say.

And in attestation of the same I repeat with heart and voice:

My God, I love Thee, not because I hope for Heaven thereby;

Nor because they who love Thee not

Must burn eternally.

Not with the hope of gaining aught,

Not seeking a reward;

But as Thyself hast loved me,

O ever–loving Lord.

IV. On the Number of the Saved

IN the three previous chapters it has been our pleasurable task to point out how beauteous is the celestial paradise, how great is the happiness enjoyed by the redeemed. And doubtless in the heart of each one of our readers a fervent desire has arisen to gain admission to the realms of eternal light, and become a partaker of its joys. Perhaps each one will feel sure that his hopes in this respect will be fulfilled.

It is, however, greatly to be feared that many a one will come short of the goal, and will be forever excluded from the kingdom of Heaven, as this chapter is intended to demonstrate. Let me, however, beg all who peruse it, not to allow what is said to discourage them, and render them pusillanimous, but rather to let it increase in them the spirit of humility and salutary fear, and stimulate them to greater energy and diligence in working out their salvation, if this appear to them less easy than they were inclined to imagine. My only motive in writing this chapter is to open the eyes of the reader, and show him his danger. For were I not to do this he might go on blindly on the wrong road, and only become aware that it is the road to perdition when it is too late to retrace his steps, when the hand of death draws the veil from his eyes. Thereupon I consider that I shall do the wanderer a service if I enlighten him as to the risk he is incurring, and endeavour to direct his steps into the path to Heaven.

Let me ask thee, O reader, what proportion thinkest thou of all who live upon this earth will be saved? Half? or a third part? or perhaps a quarter? Alas, I fear, and not without good reason, that the number will not be nearly so large. Jesus Christ, Who is eternal Truth, His holy Apostles, and the Fathers of the Church, all tell us that so it will be.

What does Christ say about the number of the elect? His words are these: "Many are called, but few are chosen." He repeats these words when He speaks of the guest who had not on a wedding garment: "Bind his hands and his feet, and cast him into the exterior darkness. For many are called, but few chosen." Were nothing more to be found to this intent in the whole of the Scriptures, this passage could not fail to alarm us. But there are many other similar ones, of which I will quote one or two.

In the Gospel of St. Matthew we read that Our Lord said: "Enter ye in at the narrow gate, for wide is the gate and broad is the way that leadeth unto destruction, and many there are that go in thereat. How narrow is the gate and strait is the way that leadeth unto life, and few there are that find it" (Matt. vii. 13). Are not these words calculated to inspire us with anxiety and apprehension? May not we be amongst those who go in at the wide gate, who walk on the broad road that ends in everlasting perdition?

In order that thou mayst better appreciate the meaning of Our Lord s words, and perceive more clearly how few are the elect, observe that Christ did not say that those were few in number who walked in the path to Heaven, but that there were but few who found that narrow way. "How strait is the gate that leadeth unto life, and few there are that find it." It is as if the Saviour intended to say: The path leading to Heaven is so narrow and so rough, it is so overgrown, so dark and difficult to discern, that there are many who, their whole life long, never find it. And those who do find it are exposed constantly to the danger of deviating from it, of mistaking their way and unwittingly wandering away from it, because it is so irregular and over grown. This St. Jerome says, in his commentary on the passage in question. Again, there are some who when they are on the right road, hasten to leave it, because it is so steep and toilsome.

There are also many who are enticed to leave the narrow way by the wiles and deceits of the devil, and thus, almost imperceptibly to themselves, are led downwards to Hell. From all that has been said we may gather that those are but few in number who find the way to Heaven, and yet fewer are those who persevere in following it unto the end.

Now because Christ knew that these words of His would be misinterpreted, and understood in a false sense by both believers and unbelievers, on another occasion He accentuated and emphasized what He had already said concerning the small number of the elect. For when one of the disciples asked Him: "Lord, are they few that shall be saved?" He answered and said: "Strive to enter by the narrow gate; for many, I say unto you, shall seek to enter and shall not be able" (Luke xiii. 24). Listen to the words of the Divine Teacher. He bids us strive, take trouble, make use of all our powers in order to enter unto the narrow gate. And what is still more calculated to appal, He adds that many shall seek to enter in and shall not be able.

If those who desire and endeavour to enter into the kingdom of Heaven fail to do so, what will be come of those who lead a careless, perhaps an ungodly life, and manifest no zeal, no interest in what concerns their eternal salvation?

We have already heard Christ three times declare to us that the number of the elect is small; that in proportion to the great mass of mankind only a few will be saved. And because He was aware that we should not lay this weighty truth to heart as we ought, He reiterates it in yet more explicit language.

After He had told a rich man who came to Him to leave all his possessions and follow Him, and the man had gone away sorrowful, He said, addressing His disciples: "How hardly shall they that have riches enter into the kingdom of God! And the disciples were astonished at His words.

But Jesus again answering saith: Children, how hard it is for them that trust in riches to enter into the kingdom of God. It is easier for a camel to pass through the eye of a needle than for a rich man to enter into the kingdom of God. Then the disciples wondered the more, saying among themselves, Who then can be saved? And Jesus looking on them saith: With men it is impossible, but not with God; for all things are possible unto God" (Mark x. 23–27).

Truly these words, coming from the lips of our Divine Master, are enough to inspire us with profound alarm; they are almost enough to cause us to despond. For they expressly tell us that the work of our salvation is a work of immense difficulty, an almost miraculous achievement, and that it is well–nigh impossible for poor humanity to enter into the kingdom of Heaven. It is in reality as much of a miracle for a man to escape everlasting perdition and to attain eternal felicity, as it would be for one man single–handed to vanquish and put to flight a whole army. For all the powers of Hell are leagued together with the wicked world against us; all the powers of Hell put their forces in array in order to conquer and enslave every one of us mortals. And with the awful powers of darkness the evil, crafty world makes common cause, and the concupiscences of the flesh do the same, for the purpose of compassing our ruin.

Now, since there are so many adversaries who assail us, adversaries so crafty, so strong, so fierce, who can deem himself sure of victory? It is little short of a miracle if one escapes the clutches of foes so numerous and so formidable. Who can hope in his own strength to triumph over them? We must needs acknowledge that all who have over come the evil enemy, the evil world, and their own evil proclivities, have been strengthened by God with His special assistance. Hence we see how toilsome and laborious a work it is to win Heaven; and we learn the truth of Our Lord's words, when He said: "The kingdom of Heaven suffereth violence, and the violent bear it away" (Matt. xi. 12).

For the consolation and encouragement of the Christian it must here be remarked that if the number of his enemies is so appallingly great, the number of his friends is still greater.

"Fear not, for there are more with us than with them." So spoke the prophet Eliseus to his frightened servant." And the Lord opened the eyes of the servant and he saw; and behold the mountain was full of horses and of chariots of fire" (4 Kings vi. 1 6). We are not left to do battle alone; our holy guardian Angel and all the blessed spirits are on our side; we may rely on the powerful protection of the Mother of God, on the virtue of the sacraments, the merits of Christ's Passion, the inspiration of the Holy Spirit, the succour of Almighty God. By means of these mighty aids we shall overcome, if we fight bravely and do not weakly yield ourselves into captivity, as unhappily too many do. For these timid, slothful, spiritless persons delude themselves with the false hope that, after all, Heaven is not hard to win. They think and say to themselves: It is not so bad a case as some would make out; Christ did not suffer for us for naught; if it were not God's will that we should be saved, He would not have created us for the enjoyment of Heaven. These and similar words we hear from the lips of the children of this world; they live according to these notions, and succeed in deceiving themselves and others.

That such persons are in error, and that they are walking on the broad road that leads to destruction, Holy Scripture leaves us no doubt.

The whole teaching of the Gospel is wholly at variance with the principles they follow; and those who live a careless life and indulge their senses are repeatedly warned that eternal death will be their portion. Listen to the admonition Christ addresses to the votaries of this world and the lovers of its luxuries: " Woe to you that are rich, for you have your consolation. Woe to you that are filled, for you shall hunger; woe to you that now laugh, for you shall mourn and weep. Woe to you when men shall bless you," that is, when men of bad principles, opposed to the maxims of religion, applaud your words, your actions, your opinions. This denunciation from Our Lord s lips may well fill us with dismay.

What object in life have the great majority of mankind? What is it that they strive after and crave for?

They desire to be rich, to be prosperous, to live in luxury, and to be praised by their fellow–men. Nobody considers this to be a sin. And yet Our Lord declares that everlasting death will be the doom of such persons, and He denounces them in forcible language.

From these and similar passages, which abound in Holy Scripture, thou seest that God is more Strict than thou dost imagine, and it is a more easy matter to lose thy soul than thou perhaps thinkest. Wherefore do not any longer live so heedlessly, but work out thy salvation with fear and trembling, as the Apostle exhorts thee. The Saints did so at all times, having the fear of God s judgments ever be fore their eyes. The ungodly, on the contrary, were ever wont to say, as many do at the present day: God is merciful, He will not condemn us so lightly to eternal damnation. But remember what is said in Holy Scripture: "Be not without fear about sin forgiven, and add not sin to sin. And say not, The mercy of the Lord is great, He will have mercy on the multitude of my sins. For mercy and wrath come quickly from Him, and His wrath looketh upon sinners" (Ecclus. v. 5–7).

We also find St. Catharine of Siena saying: "O unhappy sinners, do not rely upon the greatness of God's mercy ; believe me, the more you provoke the anger of this merciful God by willful sin, the deeper you will be cast into the abyss of perdition."

It is undoubtedly true that we ought to place our trust in God s mercy; but what the nature of our confidence should be, we are taught by St. Gregory. He says: "Let him who does all that he can, rely firmly upon the mercy of God. But for him who does not do all that lies within his power to rely upon the mercy of God would be simple presumption." To each and all of us the Apostle Peter says: "Labour the more, that by good works you may make your calling and election sure" (2 Pet. i. 10).

Several of the Fathers of the Church consider that from the fact that at the time of the deluge only eight persons were saved, at the destruction of Sodom and Gomorrah only four namely, Lot, his wife and his two daughters escaped with their lives, and of the six hundred thousand able men who departed out of Egypt not more than two reached the Promised Land, the others all dying in the desert, it may be concluded that the number of the elect amongst Christians will be proportionately small. This agrees with what St. John Chrysostom said on one occasion when he was preaching in the city of Antioch: "What think you, my hearers, how many of the inhabitants of this city may perhaps be saved? What I am about to say is very terrible, yet I will not conceal it from you. Out of this thickly populated city with its thousands of inhabitants not a hundred will be saved; I even doubt whether there will be as many as that. For what indifference we see amongst the aged, what wickedness amongst the young, what impiety amongst all classes of people."

Such words as these may well make us tremble. We should hesitate to believe them, did they not come from the lips of so great a Saint and Father of the Church. And if it is true that in the first five centuries, when the zeal and devotion of Christians was much more fervent than it is now, so small a number attained everlasting salvation, what will it be in our own day, when crime and vice prevail to so fearful an extent?

Since it is impossible for any one to deny, or even to doubt, that the number of the elect is small in proportion to that of the reprobate, I beseech thee,

O Christian reader, exert thyself to the utmost to accomplish the work of thy salvation. Thou knowest what an awful thing it is to be damned eternally.

On the Number of the Saved.

The plagues and torments of Hell are so terrible that words cannot be found to describe them. Consider in time the eternity of those unspeakable tortures, and take heed, lest thou too be cast into the abyss of never–ending anguish.

How wouldst thou be able to endure torments so immeasurable, so endless? Wouldst thou not despond and despair, wouldst thou not storm and rage? Yet that would avail thee nothing; it would only add to thy sufferings and increase thy misery.

All this is most terrible, most awful, most appalling. How is it that thou dost not think about it more often? How is it possible that thou canst live on so heedlessly? How is it possible that thou hast not more fear of Hell? Dost thou perhaps think thyself secure of Heaven? How is it that thou dost go with the multitude, as if thou didst not know that thou art in great danger of perishing with the multitude?

If thou wouldst be saved, follow the counsel of St. Anselm, when he says: "If thou wouldst be certain of being in the number of the elect, strive to be one of the few, not of the many. And if thou wouldst be quite sure of thy salvation, strive to be among the fewest of the few; that is to say: Do not follow the great majority of mankind, but follow those who enter upon the narrow way, who renounce the world, who give themselves to prayer, and who never relax their efforts by day or by night, that they may attain everlasting felicity."

CONCLUSION

Let us, my dear reader, courageously and cheer fully do all, undertake all, sacrifice all that we may gain the ineffable happiness of Heaven, for we never can purchase Heaven at too dear a price. Let us not be disheartened at the difficulties on our road, for, after all, it is not so difficult to merit Heaven. Were we to do for Heaven half as much as people do to earn a living, to acquire a little wealth, power or fame, or to enjoy life, we would be sure of securing a high place among the Saints. All we have to do to gain Heaven is to keep the commandments of God and of His Church, to bear our little crosses, to discharge the obligations of our state of life, to overcome temptation; and although this is above our natural strength, we nevertheless can count on the grace of God, if we pray earnestly for it, and with God s help everything will become comparatively easy, for, as St. Paul says: "I can do all things in Him who strengtheneth me" (Phil. iv. 13). Earnest, persistent prayer will secure Heaven to us.

I now, dear reader, address to you the words the mother of the Machabees addressed to her youngest son, a mere boy, when he was about to be tortured to death, as his six brothers had been before him: "My son, I beg thee to look up to Heaven." Look up to Heaven every day, especially in time of trial and temptation. Heaven is well worth every suffering and every sacrifice and every combat required of us, and even a thousand times more! Life is short; its trials, its sufferings, its labours, its combats, its crosses also are short and transitory; but Heaven and its joys are inconceivable, satiating every desire of the heart and never–ending!" Our present momentary and light tribulation worketh above measure exceedingly an eternal weight of glory" (2 Cor. iv. 17).

May God in His mercy grant this happy end to the writer of this book and all into whose hands it may fall.

Printed in Great Britain
by Amazon

49372421R00064